Children's
ANIMAL
Encyclopedia

Bath · New York · Singapore · Hong Kong · Cologne · Delhi · Melbourne

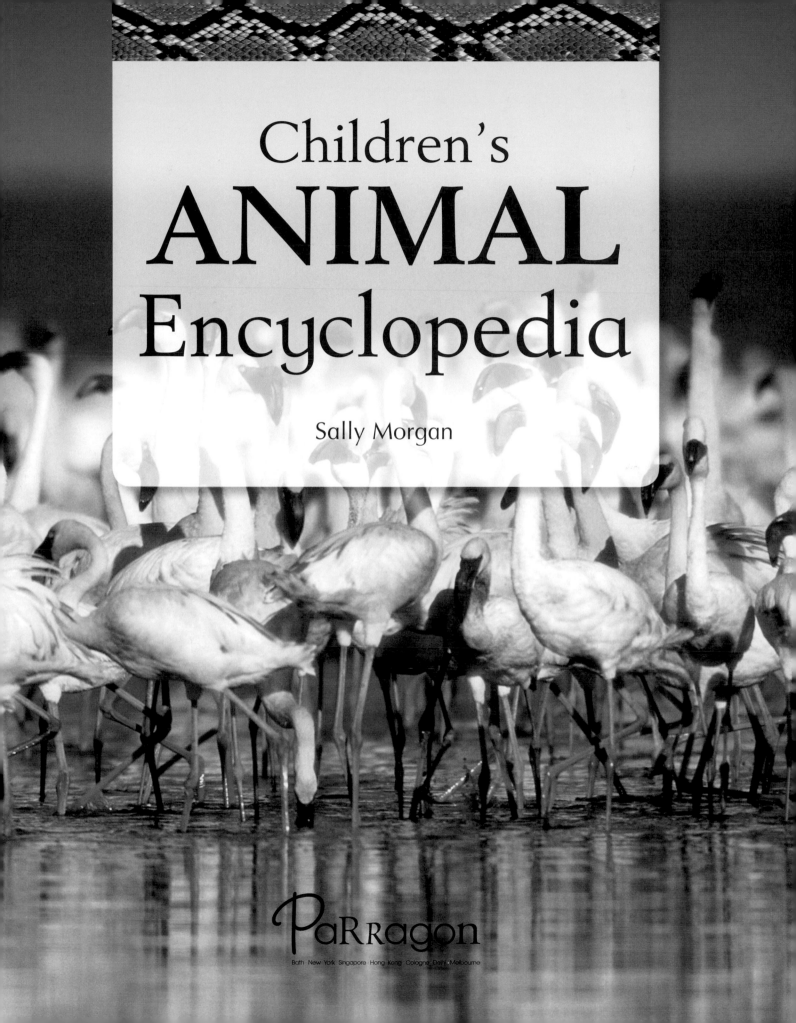

Children's
ANIMAL
Encyclopedia

Sally Morgan

PaRragon

Bath · New York · Singapore · Hong Kong · Cologne · Delhi · Melbourne

Author: Sally Morgan
Consultant: Mandy Holloway
This edition produced by Tall Tree Ltd., London

First published by Parragon in 2007

Parragon
Queen Street House
4 Queen Street
Bath BA1 1HE, UK

ISBN 978-1-4054-9454-0

Printed in Malaysia

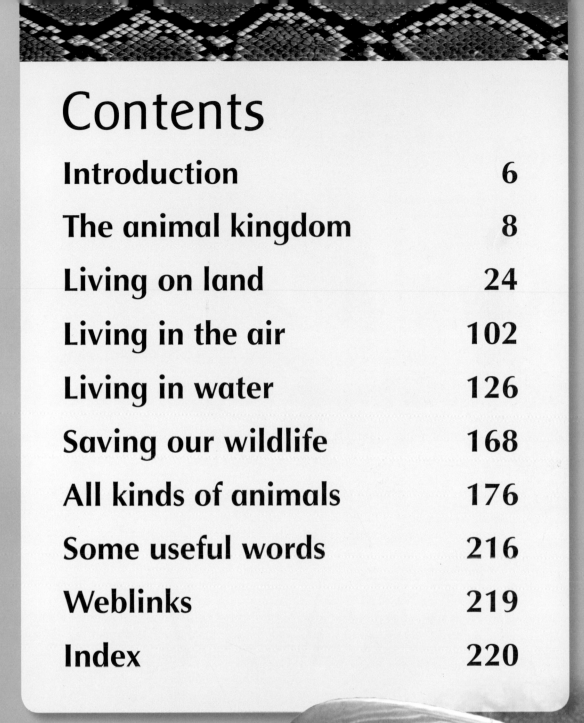

Contents

Introduction

Animals are found in every part of the world, from the warm rain forests to the freezing poles, and from high mountains to the deepest oceans.

This book tells you all about the amazing world of animals. You can read about the many different places where animals live, and find out how animals survive in their surroundings. You can also learn how many animals are under threat and what we can do to help them.

At the back of the book is a section where you can compare the different kinds of animals. There is also a list of useful words that will help you to understand any difficult words, as well as helpful web sites where you can find more information on animals and their habitats.

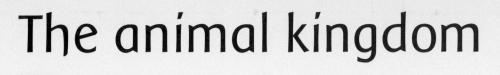

The animal kingdom

There are more than one-and-a-half million different types, or species, of animal in the world—and there are millions more still waiting to be discovered. Animals come in many different shapes, sizes, and colors. They live in a lot of different places and behave in very different ways. The largest animal is the gigantic blue whale, but some animals are as small as tiny specks of dust.

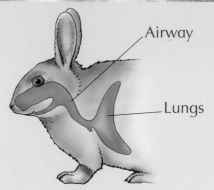

Airway

Lungs

Breathing

Many animals breathe using lungs. When this rabbit breathes in, it pulls air down its airway into its lungs.

Animal features

Animals may look very different, but they are alike in many ways. They all breathe, feed, and grow. Most animals have senses so that they can see, smell, hear, taste, and touch what is around them.

Feeding

Plants can make their own food but animals have to find something to eat. Animals that eat plants are called herbivores. Animals that eat other animals are called carnivores.

This heron is a carnivore. It feeds on small animals, such as fish.

10

Moving around

Animals move in different ways. They walk on land, fly in the air, or swim in water. Animals move to find food, to escape from a hunter, or to find a partner.

DID YOU KNOW?

The Atlantic giant squid has the largest eyes in the world. Each eyeball can measure up to 16 inches across.

Fish use fins to steer in the water.

Raising young

Animals have many different ways of having babies. Some give birth to live young, while others, such as birds and reptiles, lay eggs from which the young hatch.

The senses

Animals use their senses of sight, hearing, smell, taste, and touch to hunt for food, defend themselves, and to detect the world around them. For example, owls have large eyes that they use to hunt for prey at night.

Body parts

Animals can be divided into two groups. One group of animals has a backbone. These animals are called vertebrates. A backbone is like a stiff rod that runs down the back of a body. The other group is the invertebrates—these animals do not have backbones.

These bones are from the skeleton of a bird.

Skull

Skeletons

Fish, amphibians, reptiles, birds, and mammals are all vertebrates. Their bones make up the skeleton. The skeleton supports the animal's body and the muscles that are used to move around.

Jellyfish

Jellyfish are invertebrates that live in water. When they are out of water, jellyfish collapse into a wobbly lump of jelly.

Protected by a shell

A snail is an invertebrate. It has a shell that protects its soft body. The snail moves along using its large foot.

A snail's foot runs along the bottom of its body.

Tough armor

Crabs are invertebrates and belong to a group of animals called arthropods. Arthropods are protected by a tough outer covering called an external skeleton. Other arthropods include insects, spiders, and lobsters.

Backbone

Body organs

An organ is a part of an animal's body that has a particular job to do. For example, the eyes are used to see and the heart pumps the blood around the body. Like other animals, the human body contains many different organs, including the heart, lungs, liver, and brain.

Brain

Heart

Lungs

Liver

Stomach

Intestines

13

Animal behavior

Everything that an animal does is part of its behavior. Some behavior has to be learned, either by watching a parent or by the animal trying something for itself.

Communicating with sound

Many animals use sound to communicate with each other. An animal, such as a lion or a wolf, may use sound to tell its rivals to stay away or to attract a partner.

Wolves howl to communicate with each other.

Using color

Some animals use bright colors to attract a partner. Male peacocks have brightly colored tail feathers, which they raise to form fans. Females choose the males that have the best display.

Learning behavior

Chimpanzees have learned how to use simple tools. They push long sticks into termite nests. The termites grip the sticks, then the chimpanzees pull the sticks out and eat the termites.

Hunting

Lion cubs learn how to hunt by watching their mothers. By the time they are a couple of years old, the cubs are ready to hunt on their own.

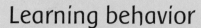

Living together

Animals that live in large groups can hunt together and protect each other. Many fish swim in large groups called shoals. All the fish within a shoal swim together, moving as if they were one.

Life cycles

Animals give birth or lay eggs to produce young animals. This is called reproduction. These young animals grow up, have young of their own, and then die. This is known as a life cycle.

Amphibians

Frogs belong to a group of animals called amphibians. They lay a mass of tiny black eggs, called frog spawn, in water. Each egg is covered in jelly.

DID YOU KNOW?

The oldest animal ever recorded was an Icelandic cyprine, which is a type of shellfish. One example lived for 374 years.

Birds

Birds lay eggs. The eggs have to be kept warm while the chicks grow inside. When the chicks are ready to hatch they use special teeth on the ends of their beaks to break out of their shells.

Budding hydras

The hydra is a simple animal that lives in water. A hydra reproduces by growing a new, identical hydra in a method called budding. A bud appears on the side of the hydra's body. This bud grows and drops off to form a new hydra.

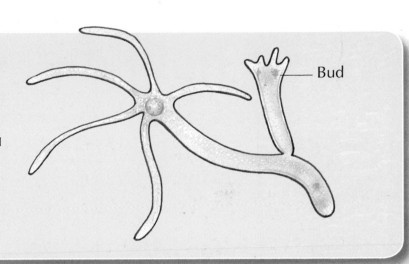

Bud

Feeding on milk

Mammals give birth to live young. After the babies are born, mammals feed their young with milk made by the mothers.

Sheep are mammals that feed milk to their young.

A long life

Some animals live for just a few days, while others will live for many years. Elephants, for example, grow very slowly and live for a long time. Some live to 80 years of age.

17

Animal habitats

The place where an animal lives is called its habitat. A habitat is made up of a community, or group, of plants and animals. There are many different types of habitat, such as mountains, seas, and cities.

The sea

The sea is the world's biggest habitat. There are deep oceans as well as shallow stretches of water near land. Animals that are found in the sea have to cope with living in salty water.

Living on mountains

Conditions on mountains change with the height. Near the peaks, it is cold and windy. Few animals live here. Lower down, there are meadows and forests where most of the animals live.

Living in cities

Many animals have moved into towns and cities. Birds nest in trees in parks and in buildings, while squirrels and foxes visit gardens and parks.

Freshwater life

Lakes and rivers are home to many different kinds of animal. These animals are used to living in freshwater, which is water that contains very little salt. They include frogs, fish, and pond snails.

A pile of logs offers animals a lot of dark places to live.

Forest homes

Woods and forests are full of trees. These offer animals a lot of places to make a home and plenty of food to eat. Even a pile of logs is home to many different animals, such as slugs, centipedes, and wood lice, as well as mice and snakes.

Food chains

All animals rely on other living things for food. Some animals eat plants, such as grass, while others hunt the plant-eating animals. This is called a food chain. Every food chain starts with plants.

Animals that only eat plants, such as antelopes, are called herbivores.

Plants

Plants are able to make their own food. They take energy from sunlight and use it to make food. They store this food in their leaves. This means that plants are full of good things for plant-eating animals to eat.

Plant eaters

The plant eaters are the first animals in the food chain. On the African plains, for example, large herds of antelope eat grass, while giraffes eat the leaves off trees.

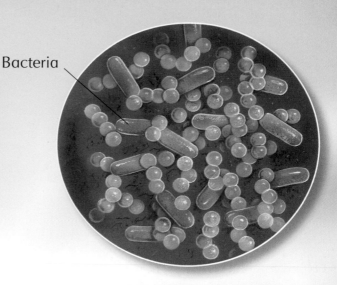

Bacteria

Meat eaters

The plant eaters are hunted by the meat eaters, or carnivores. Lions and leopards are carnivores that hunt antelopes and other grazing animals.

Animals that hunt, such as leopards, are called predators.

Recycling the waste

Bacteria break down the remains of dead animals. They recycle the bodies back into the soil to be used by plants.

Nature at risk

Sometimes, habitats are damaged by natural events, such as a drought or a fire. Today, however, a lot of damage is caused by people. Forests are cut down, grassland is plowed up, and harmful substances are pumped into the ground, air, rivers, and oceans.

Clearing trees

Each year, millions of trees in forests are cut down. Sometimes, this is to clear the land for farming or housing. This destroys animals' homes as well as the food they eat.

Too many fish

When fishermen catch too many fish in their nets, animals such as seals, sea birds, whales, and dolphins starve.

Oil spills

Large ships called tankers carry oil around the world. Occasionally, the tankers have accidents and oil spills into the sea. The oil kills sea birds and other animals.

Sea birds that are covered in oil cannot float and they quickly drown.

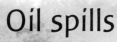

DID YOU KNOW?

The world's rain forests are being cut down so quickly that they could disappear completely in just 40 years.

Climate change

When fuels are burned they release gases into the atmosphere. These gases are thought to be changing the earth's climate and making temperatures hotter. This is called global warming.

Global warming can damage habitats and kill animals that cannot survive in the new conditions.

23

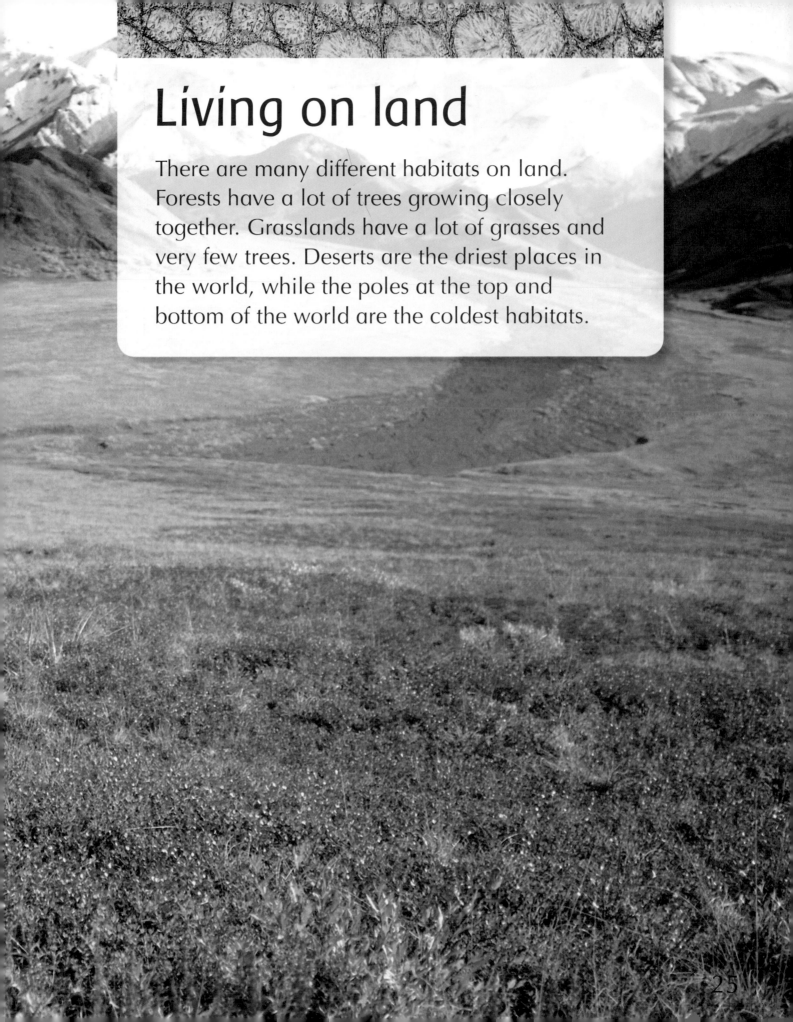

Living on land

There are many different habitats on land. Forests have a lot of trees growing closely together. Grasslands have a lot of grasses and very few trees. Deserts are the driest places in the world, while the poles at the top and bottom of the world are the coldest habitats.

Rain forests

Tropical rain forests are amazing places. They are found in the hot and wet parts of the world, close to the equator, the region around the middle of the earth. The trees grow close together and very little light reaches the forest floor.

Roof over the forest

The tops of the trees form a canopy—the "roof" of the rain forest. The canopy may be 80 to 100 feet above the ground.

Pythons coil themselves around the branches of trees when they are resting.

DID YOU KNOW?

More than half of the world's animals live in the rain forests. There are many more kinds of animal waiting to be discovered in these forests.

Hunting in trees

The python is just one of many kinds of snake that can be found living in the canopy. Pythons lie hidden in the branches waiting for their prey to pass.

26

The forest floor

Few plants are found growing on the forest floor. This is because it is too dark. The ground is covered with a layer of fallen leaves and fruit.

Roots in the air

Some plants do not grow in the soil. Instead, they grow on other plants, with their roots dangling in the air. These plants are called epiphytes. Some epiphytes produce colorful flowers that attract birds and insects.

Inside a rain forest

The plants in a rain forest grow in four layers. A few of the tallest trees poke through the rain forest canopy. Just beneath the canopy are smaller trees and shrubs. Finally, at the very bottom, is the dark forest floor.

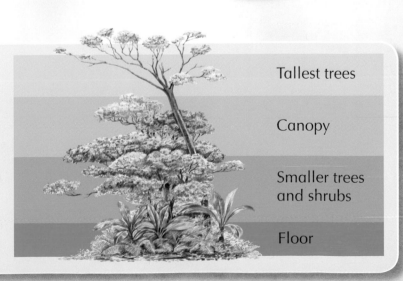

Tallest trees

Canopy

Smaller trees and shrubs

Floor

Life in the canopy

Most of the rain forest animals live in the canopy. They have learned how to move from tree to tree and where to find food and water. Some animals never come down to the ground.

Orange ape

Orangutans have long arms and legs. Their fingers are hooked to help them grip branches as they climb through the trees looking for fruit.

DID YOU KNOW?

Although most chameleons eat insects, a few species are big enough to catch and eat birds.

Colorful beak

The toucan eats fruit. It uses its long beak to reach fruit that grows at the ends of small branches.

This katydid is colored green so that it can hide among the leaves.

Insects in the canopy

Many different kinds of insect are found in the canopy where they eat leaves. These insects may be eaten by larger animals, such as birds or lizards.

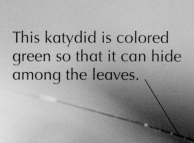

Tough beak

The scarlet macaw has a powerful hooked beak. It uses this to crack open nuts and as an extra claw to climb up the trunks of trees.

Chameleons catch insects to eat using their very long tongues.

Clever camouflage

Chameleons can change the color of their skin so that they blend in with the leaves of the trees. This is called camouflage and it makes the animals difficult to see.

Keeping in touch

Rain forests are noisy places. The trees block out much of the sunlight, so it is very gloomy. This makes it hard for animals to see each other, so they talk to each other instead.

Cicadas make a noise by vibrating thin, drumlike pieces of skin on their bodies.

Noisy cicadas

Cicadas are insects that make a deafening sound! They make these sounds when the weather changes, when they are about to mate, or if they have been disturbed.

Howling monkeys

The howler monkey is the world's loudest land-dwelling animal. Its booming call carries for up to 3 miles through the forest.

30

Frog chorus

Most rain forest frogs are active at night. This is when their croaking can be heard. The male frogs croak to attract female frogs.

When one red-eyed tree frog starts to croak, all the nearby frogs start croaking to create a deafening chorus.

Bird song

Birds sing for many reasons. Some sing to tell other birds to stay away, while others sing to attract a partner. Each kind of bird has its own song. For example, the cockatoo makes screeching and whistling sounds.

Moving around

Rain forest animals have many ways of moving around the canopy. Some run along branches and jump from tree to tree. Others swing from branch to branch, using their arms and tails.

Slow mover

Sloths move so slowly in the branches that moss and algae grow on their fur. This makes sloths slightly green in color and helps them to hide in the trees.

A spider monkey's tail is so strong that it can support the monkey's weight.

Gripping tail

The spider monkey has a long tail that it uses just like an extra leg. The monkey can wrap its tail around branches, using it to swing through the trees easily.

DID YOU KNOW?

Sloths spend most of their time hanging upside down from branches. They sleep for 15 hours a day.

Gibbons swing from one arm to the other.

Swinging around

Animals such as gibbons and spider monkeys can swing through the trees because they have very flexible shoulders. Swinging is a very fast way of getting around. The animals can move through trees faster than a human can walk on the ground.

Slithering snakes

Snakes move from one branch to another by stretching out their heads and holding on with their tails. They slither through the branches looking for birds, reptiles, and mammals to eat.

33

Rain forest floor

The rain forest floor is dark and damp. Much of it is covered in leaves, twigs, and fruit that have fallen from the trees. Few plants can survive in the gloom.

Tapirs

Tapirs are some of the largest animals that live on the forest floor. They are piglike animals with long, rubbery noses. They are found in the rain forests of Malaysia and South America.

Rotting leaves

The forest floor is covered in a thin layer of rotting leaves. Because the forest is warm and damp, the leaves rot (break down) very quickly.

Tapirs use their long noses to sniff out fallen fruit and other food.

DID YOU KNOW? A leafcutter ant can carry almost 10 times its own weight. That is like a human lifting a small car above his or her head.

Big cat

The jaguar is a large hunter that eats birds, tapirs, and even crocodiles. The dark spots on its coat help it to hide in the shadows on the forest floor.

Leafcutter ants use the pieces of leaf to grow a fungus that the ants eat.

Leafcutters

Leafcutter ants use their jaws to cut pieces of leaves to take back to their nests. Long lines of leafcutter ants can be seen in the forest, stretching from the treetops to the forest floor, where the ants have their nests.

The tiger

Tigers are the largest of all the cats. They are powerful hunters that eat pigs, deer, and young elephants. Sadly, their numbers are falling because their habitat is being destroyed and people are killing them for their fur and bones.

Canine teeth

Sharp teeth

The pointed teeth near the front of the tiger's mouth are about 4 inches long. They are called canine teeth. Tigers use their canine teeth to stab and grip prey.

Siberian tigers

Siberian tigers are the largest of all the tigers. They are found in the mountains along the border between Russia and China. Siberian tigers have thicker coats than other tigers because they have to live in very cold conditions.

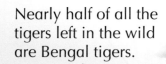

Nearly half of all the tigers left in the wild are Bengal tigers.

The Bengal tiger

Some Bengal tigers have white fur with pale stripes. Male Bengal tigers are about 10 feet long and can weigh nearly 500 pounds, or the weight of three adult humans.

Tiger cubs

A female tiger gives birth to two or three cubs. The cubs stay with their mother for about 18 months while they learn how to hunt.

Tiger facts

- 🐾 Tigers are found in India, Nepal, China, Southeast Asia, and eastern Russia.

- 🐾 In the wild, tigers can live for up to 15 years. In zoos, they will live much longer.

- 🐾 There are between 5,000 and 7,500 tigers left in the wild.

Warm grasslands

Grasslands are large areas of flat ground covered by grasses. Warm grasslands, or savannas, are found in Africa, South America, and Australia. During the dry months the grasses turn yellow. However, once the rains fall, the grasslands turn green.

A sea of grass

Some of the grasses on the savanna are taller than people. There are only a few trees, such as acacias and baobabs. Most of the young trees are eaten before they can grow very tall.

Bone-crushing hyenas

Spotted hyenas are hunters that live on the grasslands of Africa. They have strong jaws and huge teeth that can crush the bones of their prey as if they were twigs.

The great migration

Each year, huge herds of zebras and wildebeest make long journeys in search of fresh grass to eat. This is called a migration. The migration is dangerous since the animals have to cope with fast-flowing rivers and hunters, such as crocodiles.

Meerkats keep a keen eye out for hunters, such as snakes or jackals.

On guard

Meerkats live in large groups in burrows under the grasslands of southern Africa. Each member of the group has a job to do. Some are babysitters or teachers, while others are guards or hunters.

Grazing animals

The long grasses on the savanna plains attract a lot of grass-eating, or grazing, animals. When food and water are scarce, these animals join together in huge herds.

Giraffes

The giraffe has a long neck and long legs. These let it eat the leaves at the tops of trees that other animals cannot reach.

Impalas

Impalas are grazing animals that live in small herds. Green shoots of grass are their favorite food. These shoots appear soon after it rains.

40

Single toes

Zebras have long legs. These end in a single toe. The toes are protected by hard coverings called hooves.

Hoof

Large stomach

Intestines

Chewing the cud

A grazing animal swallows its food quickly when it eats. The food sits in its stomach before being brought up again into its mouth to chew. This is called chewing the cud and it helps to break up tough grass.

Waterholes

Waterholes are pools of water on the grasslands. These pools are very important because they are the only sources of drinking water during the dry season when the rains stop.

Hunters

There are many hunting animals, or predators, living on the savanna. They are attracted by the herds of grazing animals. Predators include lions, leopards, cheetahs, and birds of prey.

Running fast

The cheetah is the world's fastest runner. Its thin body and long legs are perfect for running very fast.

Working together

Lions work as a team when they hunt. Some of the lions lie in wait, while others chase an animal toward them. By hunting together, they can catch and pull down large animals, such as wildebeest.

Cheetahs use their tails for balance when they are running fast.

Birds of prey

Birds of prey look for prey while they are flying high above the ground. When they see something to eat, they swoop down on and attack the prey with their claws and beaks.

Hunting in packs

African wild dogs live together in large groups called packs. They hunt as a team and take turns chasing an animal to tire it out before catching it.

3

Termites

Termites are small insects that live together in huge groups called colonies. They build enormous nests that stretch far above and below the ground.

The worker termites that build the nests are blind.

Worker termites

Most of the termites in a colony are worker termites. These are the termites that build the nest and find food. They are just a fraction of an inch long and are a pale cream color.

Termite facts

🐾 There are more than 2,000 different species, or kinds, of termite.

🐾 Worker termites live most of their lives underground and in the nest.

🐾 Termites build their nests from clay, dirt, or wood, which they mix with saliva (liquid from their mouth).

🐾 Termites can cause a lot of damage by chewing the wood of buildings.

Towering chimneys

Termites live in large pillars called mounds. Some of the largest termite mounds rise several yards into the air. These towers are designed to let air flow freely through them to keep the nest cool.

The inside of a termite nest has thousands of tunnels and chambers.

Termites for dinner

Some animals feed on termites and can eat thousands of the insects in a day. These termite eaters include this carmine bee-eater.

Inside a nest

In addition to stretching high above the ground, termites' nests reach deep into the ground. Here, there are underground chambers where the queen termite lays her eggs and where the workers store food.

Scavengers

Animals that feed on the dead remains of other animals are called scavengers. Scavengers on the savanna include vultures, jackals, and dung beetles.

Jackals follow lions and will eat up any meat that the lions leave on a dead body.

Stealing food

Some hunters, such as this jackal, are scavengers. They have found that it is easier to eat dead animals, or to steal an animal killed by another hunter, than to kill prey themselves.

Vultures

Vultures can see a dead animal on the ground from high in the sky. They glide down to the ground and are soon joined by other vultures to pick over the body.

46

Cleaning up

Dung beetles use their sense of smell to find fresh dung on the ground. They roll the dung into a ball and push it into a hole in the ground beside their eggs. The young beetles feed on the dung when they hatch.

Keeping clean

The heads and necks of vultures are either covered in short feathers or they have no feathers at all. This allows the vultures to stick their heads right inside a dead body and not get any long feathers covered in blood.

Vultures have sharp beaks to rip meat off a dead body.

Deserts

Deserts are places that have very little rain. Some deserts are hot but there are cold deserts, too. The animals that live in deserts have to be able to survive in a dry place.

Sand dunes

Sand dunes are formed by the wind blowing the sand into piles. Some animals burrow into the dunes to escape the heat and cold.

DID YOU KNOW?

The largest hot desert in the world is the Sahara in North Africa. It is almost the same size as the United States.

The Atacama

The center of the Atacama Desert in South America is the driest place on the earth. In some parts, rain has not fallen for hundreds of years. Animals that live here are only found near the coast, where there is water.

North America

The deserts of North America have more plant life than many other deserts. These plants include small bushes and cacti. Some animals make their homes in the cacti or feed on their flowers and fruit.

The cactus stores water inside its stem.

Cold deserts

Antarctica lies around the South Pole. It is the coldest place in the world, but so little rain and snow falls that the region is called a desert. Despite this, a lot of animals visit Antarctica to feed and breed during the summer months. These include whales, penguins, and seals.

49

Locust swarms

Locusts form groups called swarms. They fly out of the desert and eat whole crops in neighboring regions.

Hot deserts

Most deserts are hot during the day, so animals creep under bushes or into holes to escape the sun. At night, the temperatures fall and it can be very cold.

The fox's large ears are very good at hearing prey running across the sand.

Nighttime hunter

Bat-eared foxes avoid the heat of the desert by sleeping in burrows during the day. They come out at night to hunt when it is cooler.

Geckos

Geckos are small lizards. They run on the tips of their feet so that they do not get burned by the hot desert sand.

Geckos lick their eyeballs to stop them from drying out.

The sting of some scorpions can kill people.

Scorpions

Some scorpions live in deserts. They are nocturnal, which means that they are active at night. They ambush prey and sting it with their tail stings before eating it.

Desert reptiles

Reptiles are animals that have a scaly skin. They include snakes and lizards. The scaly skin stops their bodies from losing too much water in the dry desert.

Thorny devils

These strange-looking lizards live in the deserts of Australia. Their bodies are covered with very sharp spines. These help to keep hunters away.

Tortoises have a thick shell to protect them from hunters.

The desert tortoise

Desert tortoises get water by eating plants. They store this water in their bodies and use it when they cannot find any plants to eat.

Poisonous rattlesnakes

Rattlesnakes are poisonous snakes that have rattles at the ends of their tails. They shake their rattles when they are threatened as a warning to other animals. Their sharp teeth inject poison when the snakes bite. This poison kills or paralyzes their prey.

Sidewinders

Sidewinders are snakes that can move over hot sand without getting burned. They move sideways, with just a few parts of their bodies touching the sand. The snakes leave behind a series of lines in the sand as their tracks.

Tracks

The camel

The camel is an expert at surviving in the desert. It can go for two weeks without water. A camel can even drink salty water that would kill other animals.

One hump

Dromedary camels are found in the hot deserts of Africa and the Middle East. They have a single hump on their backs.

Camel facts

- Camels have large, broad feet that are ideal for walking through the desert because they do not sink into the sand.

- Most people think that a camel's hump is full of water. Instead, it is full of fat. A camel uses this fat when it cannot find enough food to eat.

Bactrian camels have thick coats to keep them warm.

Two humps

Bactrian camels have two humps on their backs. They are found in the cold deserts of China and Central Asia.

A camel's ears are lined with thick hair to keep out sand.

Desert protection

The camel has long eyelashes to protect its eyes from the sun and blowing sand. Its nostrils can close shut tightly to keep out any sand.

Cool grasslands

Grasslands found in the cooler parts of the world are called temperate grasslands. These regions are warm in the summer, and they may be covered in snow in the winter.

What's in a name?

Temperate grasslands are called different names in different parts of the world. In North America, they are called prairies. In South America, they are called pampas, and in Asia, they are known as steppes.

Herd animals

Some plant-eating animals join together in huge herds, or groups, on the grasslands. These include pronghorns, which are a kind of antelope that live in North America.

56

Sharp points

Porcupines are covered in thousands of sharp spines called quills. When attacked, they turn their backs on their enemy and raise their quills to protect themselves.

Porcupine quills break off easily and remain stuck in an attacker.

Prairie hunters

There are a number of predators, or hunters, on the prairie, such as coyotes. They hunt hares and small deer, on their own or in packs. Coyotes communicate by making long, loud howls.

Grassland mammals

A lot of plant-eating mammals are attracted to grasslands because there is plenty of food. These plant eaters also attract hunters that come looking for animals to eat.

Digging hunter

The badger uses its long, sharp claws to dig small animals, such as ground squirrels and mice, out of the ground.

Rabbits thump the ground with their back legs to warn other rabbits of danger.

Good listener

The rabbit has long ears, which give it a good sense of hearing. It uses these to listen for any hunters that may be nearby.

Red fox

The red fox is a carnivore, or meat-eater. It is usually active at night, when it hunts for small mammals, such as rabbits. It also eats berries.

Pack animals

Llamas are found on the grassy slopes of the Andes Mountains in South America. These plant eaters live in groups called herds and are used by local people to carry heavy loads.

Llamas are related to camels.

59

American bison

The American bison is the largest land mammal in North America. It is easily recognized by its extra-large head and shoulders and its shaggy coat.

Keeping sharp

Both the male and female bison have a pair of short, curved horns. They rub their horns against trees or rocks to keep them sharp.

Bison use their horns to fight each other.

Bison facts

🐾 When attacked by wolves or other large hunters, bison form a circle around their young with their horns pointing outward.

🐾 Adult bison can weigh up to 2,000 pounds. That is as much as 12 adult humans.

🐾 The bison is also called the American buffalo.

DID YOU KNOW?

Bison can run very quickly. They can reach speeds of up to 45 miles per hour.

Return of the bison

During the late 1800s, human hunters killed nearly all of the bison. Only 1,000 or so survived. Today, they are protected by law and their numbers are increasing.

Surviving the cold

At the start of winter, bison move from the grasslands to valleys and wooded areas, where they can shelter from the cold winter storms.

61

Living under the grassland

A large number of animals live under grasslands. Many dig deep holes, called burrows, in the soil. Others use the holes for shelter.

Prairie dogs

Prairie dogs are named after their call, which sounds like a dog's bark. They live together in large groups and dig a maze of burrows, which is called a town.

DID YOU KNOW? One hundred years ago, there were as many as 5 billion prairie dogs living on the grasslands of North America.

Tunneling moles

Moles are small animals with large front feet that are shaped like spades. They use their feet to dig tunnels through the soil. Moles feed on worms and other small animals that fall into the tunnels.

Prairie dogs

Burrowing owl

Badger

Rabbit

Ferret

Salamander

Living in tunnels

Tunnels dug by prairie dogs and moles can be homes to other animals. These include salamanders, which are related to frogs and toads. There is even a kind of bird, called the burrowing owl, which lives in tunnels underground. Hunters also move into the burrows, such as snakes, ferrets, and badgers.

Wombats

Wombats are nighttime plant eaters that are found only in Australia. They live in burrows that can be up to 65 feet long and lie more than 6 feet below the ground.

63

Living in the trees

Many kinds of animals make their homes in trees all around the world. Trees give them both food and shelter.

Fussy eater

Koalas live in the forests of Australia and they eat only the leaves from eucalyptus trees. Koalas sleep during the day when it is hot and become active at sunset.

Koalas rarely drink water. They usually get the liquid they need from leaves.

Building a nest

Many birds make their nests from materials they find in the forests. They collect twigs, leaves, moss, feathers, and pieces of sheep's fleece to use in their nests.

Tree frogs

Most frogs live on the ground, but tree frogs live high up in rain forest trees. They have sticky pads at the tips of their toes that help them to grip branches.

Squirrels use their bushy tails to keep warm at night.

DID YOU KNOW?

Eucalyptus leaves are poisonous to most animals. But koalas can destroy the poisons inside their bodies, making the leaves safe to eat.

The red squirrel

The red squirrel has reddish brown fur and long ear tufts. It is found in northern forests and feeds on seeds and nuts.

Mixed forests

Temperate forests are found in cool parts of the world. They are a mixture of trees that lose their leaves in winter (deciduous trees) and trees that keep their leaves during the cold months (evergreen trees).

Losing leaves

Deciduous trees lose their leaves because they do not get enough water in the winter. The water in the ground freezes, making it impossible for trees to collect it through their roots. The leaves turn brown and fall off.

Millipedes eat the leaves that fall off the trees.

Living on the floor

The forest floor is covered with plants and fallen leaves. These make it an ideal home for many small animals, such as millipedes.

Forest birds

Temperate forests are home to many birds. The birds eat the seeds and fruit that grow on the trees, as well as insects living there. The birds also build nests in the branches.

Wrens hunt for insects in holes and cracks in trees.

Wild boar

Wild boar are large pigs that live in forests. They eat roots, fruit, and berries that lie on the forest floor. Male boar have curved teeth called tusks, which stick out of their mouths.

DID YOU KNOW?

The largest tree, the Sequoia, can grow to more than 325 feet tall and live for 2,000 years.

Woodland insects

Many insects lay their eggs on trees. When the eggs hatch, the young insects are then close to their favorite food—leaves.

This caterpillar is brightly colored as a warning that it is poisonous.

Caterpillars

Caterpillars are the larvae, or young, of butterflies and moths. They eat leaves and grow in size before they turn into adult moths and butterflies.

Some caterpillars look like small twigs.

Clever hiders

Many caterpillars are difficult to see on trees. Some are colored green so that they blend in with the leaves. This makes them hard for hunters to see.

68

Insect hunters

The insects living among the leaves attract many woodland birds, such as blue tits. These birds pick the insects out of the bark on the trees. They eat the insects or feed them to their young.

Blue tits build their nests inside holes in tree trunks.

All about galls

Galls are small balls that grow on leaves and branches. The galls are made by insects called gall wasps. The wasps lay their eggs inside a leaf or branch. As the egg hatches and the young wasp grows, the plant swells to form a gall with the insect inside.

Young wasp

69

Woodland floor

The woodland floor is damp and shady and is covered in a thick layer of leaves and twigs. Many animals live here, hiding from hunters and looking for something to eat.

Stag beetles

Young stag beetles, or larvae, grow up on the forest floor. The adult males have huge jaws, which they use to fight each other.

DID YOU KNOW?

When two male stag beetles fight, the winner is the beetle that can flip its opponent over.

Woodland mice

During the day, woodland mice hide in small tunnels to avoid hunters. At night, they come out and look for seeds, fruit, nuts, and small insects to eat.

70

Wolf spiders bite
their prey with their
huge fangs.

Wolf spiders

Unlike many other spiders, wolf spiders do not
make webs. Instead, they chase their prey on
the ground. When they catch an animal, they
inject it with poison so that it stops moving.

Woodcocks use their long
bills to pick earthworms
out of the soil.

Ground nesting

The woodcock nests on
the woodland floor. The
female bird has patchy
colored feathers that
blend with the dead
leaves on the ground.
This hides her when
she is on the nest.

Surviving winter

Winter is a difficult time for animals. There is little food to eat and water can be frozen solid. Animals find different ways of surviving the cold winter months.

Storing squirrels

During the fall, squirrels bury food, such as nuts, in the ground. In the winter, they dig the nuts up again to eat.

Woodland deer

Deer shelter in woodlands throughout the winter, nibbling the buds off the ends of branches. They also push snow to one side with their feet so that they can find food.

Sleeping skunks

Striped skunks go to sleep for several days at a time during the winter. On milder winter days, they wake up and hunt for food.

Skunks protect themselves by spraying a smelly liquid at attackers.

Hibernation

Some animals, such as dormice, survive the winter by crawling into a safe place and going into a very deep sleep. This is called hibernation. The animals wake up when the weather gets warmer in spring.

Migrating birds

Birds such as swallows avoid the cold weather by flying to warmer parts of the world. Once the winter has finished and the weather gets warmer, the birds fly back. This journey is called a migration.

DID YOU KNOW?

As deer's antlers grow, they become covered in a furry skin called velvet.

Northern forests

A band of evergreen forest stretches across the top of North America, Europe, and Asia. The trees that grow here are called conifers. Winters are long and cold, and there are fewer animals than in warmer forests because there is little food to eat.

Grazing deer

Large deer live in the northern coniferous forests, feeding off grass, twigs, and bark. Some deer grow enormous antlers on top of their heads. At the end of each year, these antlers drop off and new ones start to grow.

Male white-tailed deer use their antlers to fight each other in the fall. This is called rutting.

Sharp leaves

Conifer trees have leaves shaped like needles. These leaves are very sharp, and they are not very good for animals to eat.

Laying eggs

The wood wasp, or horntail, lays its eggs in the bark of conifer trees. The female has a long, pointed tube at the end of her body, which she digs into the bark to lay her eggs.

Egg-laying tube

Team birds

The northern forests are home to many birds. This blue jay lives in forests in North America. Blue jays will work together and attack other animals that get too near their nests.

Forest hunters

The lynx is one of the hunting animals that live in the northern forests. It climbs up a tree and waits for an animal to pass close by before leaping down and attacking.

The brown bear

Brown bears are found in Europe, Asia, and North America. They live in forests, grasslands, and on mountains. They have thick, furry coats that are gray, brown, or even black in color.

Brown bear facts

🐾 Bears can run at speeds of up to 35 miles per hour.

🐾 Brown bears are omnivorous. This means that they will eat any kind of food, including meat and plants.

🐾 Male brown bears are much larger than female bears. In some cases, the male can be twice as large as the female.

Large animals

The largest brown bears are found on Kodiak Island in Alaska. They can weigh more than 1,300 pounds—that is as much as nine adult humans!

76

Catching salmon

In the fall, brown bears feast on salmon. They stand in rivers and catch the fish with their jaws and long claws.

Some bears stand on top of waterfalls and catch salmon as they jump up.

A mouthful of teeth

Bears use their teeth to catch prey, and also to attack other bears. They have a pair of long, sharp teeth at the front of their mouths for gripping animals.

Looking for food

Bears will eat anything! They will even raid human campsites and trash cans looking for something to eat.

Birds of the forest

Mixed forests are home to a lot of different birds. These birds shelter and nest in the trees. Some only visit the forests in the winter, but others stay all year round.

Woodpeckers

Woodpeckers make their nests in holes in tree trunks. They hammer their strong beaks against the trunks to dig out the holes.

DID YOU KNOW?

Woodpeckers have four toes on their feet. Two point forward and two point backward. This helps them to climb up and down tree trunks easily.

Ghost of the forest

The great gray owl has gray feathers with black and white spots. These make the owl look like it is a ghost.

Wild turkeys

Wild turkeys live in forests in North America. They spend most of their time on the ground, but they can fly over 500 yards to escape an attacker.

Turkeys have small, weak wings, so they can fly only short distances.

Goshawks eat rabbits and squirrels.

Goshawks

The goshawk is a bird of prey—that is, a bird that hunts other animals. Goshawks have very good eyesight and can see their prey from high up in the sky.

79

Frozen wastes

North of the coniferous forests lies an icy wasteland called the tundra. This region is frozen throughout the winter, but bursts into life when the snow melts in the short summer months.

Fierce wolverines

The wolverine looks like a small bear, but it is related to the weasel. It lives in the northern forests and the tundra and has a thick coat of fur to protect it from the cold.

Always frozen

Just beneath the surface of the tundra, the soil is always frozen. This stops plants with large roots, such as trees, from growing there. But during the summer, small plants, such as this Arctic poppy, burst into bloom.

Tundra plains

When the summer arrives, the snow melts and forms pools on the tundra's surface. The soil becomes soft enough for small animals to burrow into, seeking shelter or food.

Snow geese

Snow geese fly to the tundra in the summer to raise their young. In the fall, they fly south to warmer areas.

Snow geese fly in large flocks, or groups.

Herds of reindeer

Reindeer move into the tundra in the summer to give birth to their young. When winter comes, the reindeer herds return to the coniferous forests.

DID YOU KNOW?

The Arctic tundra covers one-tenth of the earth's total surface.

81

The Arctic

The Arctic is the region around the North Pole. This icy world has very long winters. In the middle of winter, the sun sets and does not rise again for several weeks.

Changing ice sheet

The Arctic is covered by a thick sheet of ice. During the summer, some of the ice melts and the sheet gets smaller. This means that land hunters, such as polar bears, have less area to hunt in, and they can struggle to find food.

Keeping warm

Seals have a thick layer of fat, called blubber, just beneath their skin. This keeps the seals warm in the icy Arctic seas.

Multicolored beaks

Puffins catch small fish to eat and to feed to their young. They hold the fish in their colorful beaks and carry about 10 fish at a time.

DID YOU KNOW?

Puffins are very good swimmers and can dive to depths of 200 feet to look for fish.

A new coat

The Arctic fox changes the color of its coat during the year to blend in with its surroundings. In winter, it has a white coat to hide in the snow. In summer, it turns brown to match the rocks and soil.

Traveling animals

During the summer, many animals travel to the Arctic to feed and breed. When it gets colder in the fall, they move away again. This journey is called migration.

Huge herds of caribou travel hundreds of miles to the tundra and back.

Migrating caribou

Caribou are a kind of deer that live in North America. They spend the winter in the forests, but move north in summer to give birth to their calves and to feed on the Arctic tundra.

Hunting wolves

Wolves follow the caribou on their migration, hunting the older and weaker animals. They are very good runners and will follow herds of caribou for up to 13 miles every day.

DID YOU KNOW?

An Arctic tern can live for 20 years. This means that one tern may fly around the world 20 times during its lifetime.

Record traveler

Arctic terns make the longest migration of any animal. They breed in the Arctic in summer and fly to the Antarctic for winter, before returning to the Arctic. That is a round-trip journey of at least 20,000 miles.

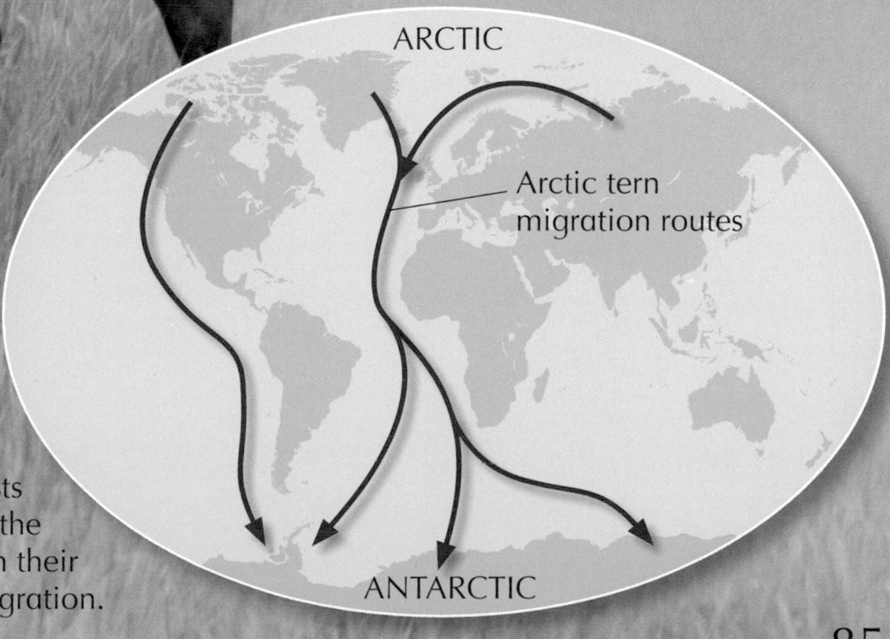

ARCTIC

Arctic tern migration routes

Arctic terns follow the coasts of Europe, Africa, or the Americas on their long migration.

ANTARCTIC

The polar bear

Polar bears are the world's largest land hunters. They usually live on their own, prowling over the Arctic ice looking for seals to eat.

Polar bears have even caught beluga whales to eat.

Fur coat

Polar bears have thick coats of white fur so that they blend in with the snow and cannot be seen by their prey. Beneath the fur is a thick layer of fat. The fur and fat help to keep the polar bear warm.

Too hot!

The fur and fat on polar bears are so good at trapping heat that the animals can get too warm in the summer. They have to lie down on the ice to cool off.

Bear watching

Watching polar bears is very popular in Canada. People use special vehicles so that they can get close to the animals.

Polar bear facts

🐾 The soles of a polar bear's feet are very rough. This stops the bear from slipping around on the ice.

🐾 Adult male polar bears can weigh up to 1,500 pounds— that is about the weight of 10 adult humans.

🐾 When it is very cold, some polar bears cover their faces to stop their bodies from losing heat through their noses.

Strong swimmers

Polar bears are excellent swimmers, using their large feet to paddle through the icy water. Some bears have been seen swimming 60 miles from land.

Antarctica

Antarctica is the region around the South Pole. Unlike the Arctic, there is a large amount of land in Antarctica, which is covered by thick ice. These cold conditions make life very harsh for the animals living here.

Food for all

Many animals visit Antarctica in the summer. Tiny plants and animals in the sea, called plankton, increase in number as the weather gets warmer. The plankton attract fish, which provide food for seals and penguins.

Leopard seals

Leopard seals are fierce hunters. In addition to eating fish and squid, they also eat penguins and other seals.

Polar tourists

Very few people live in Antarctica, but more and more people are visiting the region as tourists. These tourists need to be very careful that they do not damage the area by dropping litter or disturbing the animals.

Swimming birds

Many penguins lay their eggs and raise their young in Antarctica. They warm their eggs in folds of skin by their feet.

Chinstrap penguins are named after the thin band of black feathers that runs under their chins.

Penguins

Penguins are swimming birds that live in the earth's southern hemisphere (the southern half of our planet). They have webbed feet and flipperlike wings, which they use to swim.

Keeping warm

Unlike other birds, penguins have feathers all the way down their legs. They also have a thick layer of fat under their skin. These help to keep them warm in the cold Antarctic.

Emperor penguins take good care of their young.

Penguin facts

- Emperor penguins are the largest penguins. They can weigh nearly 100 pounds—that is the weight of 20 large bags of flour!
- The largest penguin colonies can contain more than 10 million birds.

Huge colonies

When it is time to breed, penguins gather together in large groups called colonies. They huddle together to keep each other warm.

The jackass penguin

Jackass penguins get their name from the loud braying noise that they make, which sounds like a donkey. They are found on the beaches of southern Africa.

Flying underwater

Penguins are clumsy on land but are graceful and fast in water. The surface of their bodies is smooth so that they slip through the water easily. They find it difficult to walk on land and often slide along the snow on their bellies.

Jackass penguins are about 27 inches tall and weigh up to 9 pounds.

91

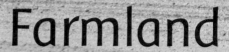

Farmland

Large areas of land have been cleared around the world to make space for farms. Wild animals come to this farmland to eat the crops, or to hunt smaller animals.

Farming fields

Farmland has a mixture of habitats. There may be shrubs between the fields and small pockets of woodland. There are also meadows, which are fields where farm animals graze. These are often full of wild flowers.

Butterfly meadows

Meadows are important habitats for insects. In early summer, the grasses are tall and there are lots of flowers, which attract butterflies and bees.

This red admiral butterfly feeds on nectar, a sugary liquid in flowers.

Farm animals

People have been farming animals, such as cows, sheep, and pigs, for thousands of years. We farm these animals because we can use the milk, meat, and wool that they produce.

Bumblebees

Bumblebees visit the flowers that grow in meadows and shrubs. They collect nectar and carry it back to their hives, or nests. They use the nectar to make honey, which they eat in winter.

DID YOU KNOW?

Bees will fly up to 9 miles from their hives in search of flowers.

Seed eaters

Farmland is good for birds because it provides plenty of food. Seed-eating birds, such as goldfinches, have short, strong beaks that are ideal for cracking open seeds.

Living in cities

Many animals live close to people—in parks and yards, in homes, and under the ground in sewers. These animals include foxes, squirrels, rats, and pigeons.

City homes

Cities make ideal homes for some animals. There are a lot of places to shelter or build nests. There is plenty of food, too. This can be found in trash cans, in litter on the streets, and in homes.

Foxes are related to dogs and wolves.

Urban foxes

The red fox has gotten used to living close to people. It visits yards at night, and finds food in trash cans.

Racoons

Racoons are found in North America where they often visit yards and parks. These clever animals use their long fingers to open bags and boxes to get at any food inside.

Falcons eat other birds and small mammals, such as mice.

City pigeons

Pigeons are a common sight in many cities. They gather together in parks and other open spaces looking for food. They can be a nuisance because their droppings make a lot of mess.

Nesting falcons

Peregrine falcons build their nests on high buildings. From here, they have a good view of any prey moving around below.

95

Living in caves

Many caves are cold and damp and often lie far below ground. Very little light can reach these places. The animals that live there have to cope with complete darkness.

Bat caves

Bats sleep, or roost, in caves during the day, hanging upside down with their claws gripping the cave walls. At night, they fly out of the caves to hunt for food.

Caves

Caves range in size from small hollows in a cliff to enormous cave networks that are hundreds of miles long.

No eyes

The blind cave fish has no eyes. This is not a problem because the caves are dark, so the fish does not need to see. Instead, it relies on its other senses to move around and find food.

Cave spiders

Cave spiders are very common in many parts of the world. They lay their eggs in large sacs shaped like teardrops, which hang from the cave roof.

Cave spiders hunt small insects and woodlice.

DID YOU KNOW?

The tiny tooth cave spider is about the size of one of these letters. This minute hunter spins webs on the walls of caves in Texas.

Eagle's nest

Golden eagles build huge eyries, or nests, on cliffs and mountains. They are strong hunters, catching mice, hares, and even deer.

Mountains

Mountains have many different kinds of habitat. There are thick rain forests and meadows, as well as steep slopes covered in rocks and fast-flowing streams.

Golden eagles glide on wings that can measure 8 feet across.

Changing habitats

Habitats on a mountain change with the altitude, or height. At the bottom there are forests. Higher up, the trees stop and are replaced by grasslands. At the very top, there are a few small plants and little else.

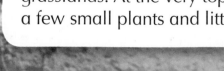

Mountain gorilla

Mountain gorillas are found in rain forests in the mountains of central Africa. They have thick coats that help them stay warm during the cold mountain nights.

DID YOU KNOW?

Snow leopards wrap their long, thick tails around their faces to keep their noses and lungs warm at night.

Mountain hunters

Snow leopards are found in the mountains of Asia. They are strong hunters that usually hunt sheep and goats. Once snow leopards have killed their prey, they stay close to the body to stop other animals from stealing it.

Snow leopards are strong enough to kill prey three times their size.

Life on rocks and snow

Few animals can survive at the tops of mountains. There is very little to eat and the ground is covered in large, slippery boulders. Temperatures are low and snow lies on the ground all year round.

Mountain movers

Bighorn sheep move up mountains during the summer to feed on grasses on the high slopes. When winter comes, they move down again to escape the snow.

DID YOU KNOW?

Mountain goats can leap 10 feet from one ledge to another. They can also turn around on ledges that are only a few inches wide.

Bighorn sheep like open ground, where they can easily see any attackers.

100

Yaks

The yak is a large, shaggy animal that lives in the Himalaya Mountains in Asia. It has a thick coat to keep it warm in the cold mountain air.

Sure-footed goats

Mountain goats are found on the steepest cliffs, where they leap from ledge to ledge. They can do this because they have special hooves that grip the rock.

The name marmot comes from an old French word meaning "mountain mouse."

Whistling warning

Marmots are small animals that live in large groups on mountain slopes. Their warning call is a high-pitched whistle. When other marmots hear this whistle, they know danger is near and run into their burrows.

101

Living in the air

Many animals have learned how to fly through the air. These include birds, insects, and bats. They fly using wings made from feathers or flaps of skin, which they flap to lift them off the ground. Flying lets these animals hunt for food in the air and helps them escape from predators.

Birds

Birds are animals that are covered in feathers. These keep them warm and help them fly. Birds also have wings instead of arms, and a hard bill, or beak, which they use to collect food.

Hunting birds

Birds that hunt other animals are called birds of prey. They have large hooked beaks and huge claws, called talons, which they use to catch their food.

Buzzards fly high in the air keeping an eye out for prey.

Kingfishers use their long bills to catch fish.

Colorful feathers

Some birds, such as kingfishers, have very bright and colorful feathers. This is usually to attract a partner. Birds will sometimes perform a special dance to make themselves look even more attractive.

104

Waterproof feathers

Birds that live in water, such as ducks, have oily feathers. This stops water from soaking into their feathers. Otherwise the birds would sink.

Mallards are sometimes called dabbling ducks because they dabble, or dip, for pondweed.

DID YOU KNOW?

The peregrine falcon is the fastest animal in the world. When it dives down to catch its prey, it can reach speeds of up to 170 miles per hour.

Preening

Birds look after their feathers by keeping them clean. This is called preening. They use their beaks to straighten any bent feathers.

Birds' wings

Birds have wings instead of arms. They fly by extending and flapping their wings. The wings are made from a number of bones with feathers attached to them. They can be long and broad or short and narrow.

Gliding through air

Gliding birds, such as gannets, use rising air, or currents, to fly. These birds have very large wings that catch the currents and carry the birds into the air.

Some gannets have wings that measure nearly 6 feet across.

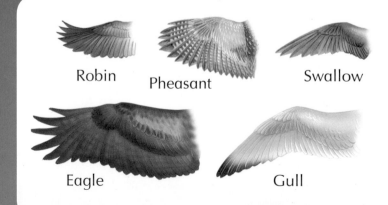

Wing shapes

Robin Pheasant Swallow

Eagle Gull

Birds that fly by gliding and soaring, such as eagles and gulls, have large wings with long feathers. Birds that fly short distances and need to dart about quickly, such as robins, pheasants, and swallows, have short wings, which they flap quickly.

Silent fliers

Some owls do not make a sound when they fly. They have soft feathers along the fronts of their wings, which quiet the sound of the air as it passes over the wings.

Fast flight

Swallows have short wings that let them fly quickly and dart about to catch flying insects. If they need to dive, they pull their wings into their bodies and drop like a stone.

Some hummingbirds flap their wings 1,200 times a minute.

Hovering hummingbirds

Hummingbirds are small birds that can hover. They stay in one place by beating their wings backward and forward very quickly. This allows them to hover in front of a flower so that they can reach in and drink nectar.

The bald eagle

Bald eagles are birds of prey. This means that they eat other animals. They have very good eyesight, which they use to spot their prey far below.

Large wingspan

Bald eagles have a wingspan of over 8 feet. They use their large wings to catch rising currents of warm air and soar high into the sky.

Eagle food

Bald eagles eat small birds, fish, and mammals. They will also eat dead animals, especially in winter, when living food is hard to find.

A bald eagle catches a fish with its sharp claws. These claws are called talons.

DID YOU KNOW? The name "bald eagle" does not mean that the bird has no feathers on its head. Instead, the word "bald" in old English meant "white."

Eagle facts

- An adult female bald eagle weighs just under 13 pounds, while the male weighs nearly 9 pounds.

- Bald eagles live for about 25 years in the wild, but up to 50 years in captivity.

- Young bald eagles are completely brown. The white head feathers do not appear until the bird is four years old.

Nesting eagles

Bald eagles build huge nests called eyries. A pair of eagles always uses the same nest, making it bigger each year. An eagle's nest can weigh more than 1,000 pounds, or the weight of six adult humans.

Hooked beaks

Bald eagles have a large hooked beak. They use this to rip their prey to pieces and tear off chunks of meat to swallow.

Flightless birds

Flightless birds have feathers and wings but cannot fly. They include the largest birds in the world, such as ostriches, rheas, and emus.

Ostriches live on the hot grasslands of Africa.

Fast runners

Ostriches have long, powerful legs, which they use to run away from hunters. They can reach speeds of 40 miles per hour.

Cormorants

The flightless cormorant is a bird that lives in the Galapagos Islands. It swims through the sea around the coast, catching fish, squid, and octopus to eat.

Kiwis are about the same size as a chicken.

A cassowary has a large bony growth called a casque.

Kiwis of New Zealand

Kiwis live in the forests, swamps, and grasslands of New Zealand. They are named after their unusual call, which is a high-pitched whistle. Kiwis have nostrils at the ends of their long beaks, which they use to sniff out insects.

Cassowary

Cassowaries live in the rain forests of Australia. These tall birds have a razor-sharp claw on the end of each leg, which they use to defend themselves.

111

Building nests

Most birds build nests in which they lay their eggs. Different birds build different-shaped nests, which range from simple cup shapes to enormous platforms.

Building materials

Nests are made from a range of materials, such as twigs, leaves, moss, wool, and feathers. Some birds even use human garbage to build their nests.

This paradise flycatcher has made its nest from twigs, leaves, and moss.

Swallow nests

Swallows build their nests out of small balls of mud and clay. Each nest can contain 1,500 balls of clay.

DID YOU KNOW?

The vervain hummingbird builds the smallest bird's nest, which is about the size of half a walnut shell.

Weaving a nest

Weaver birds build their nests by weaving thin twigs and reeds together. Woven nests usually have narrow entrances to stop egg-eating animals from getting inside.

Massive platforms

Some birds, such as storks and eagles, build large platform nests out of sticks and twigs. The largest platforms can measure more than 6 feet across and 20 feet deep.

A spectacled weaver bird stands at the narrow entrance to its nest.

Small birds, such as blue tits, are safe from hunters in a nest box.

Nest boxes

A good way to attract birds into the yard is to put up a nest box. Birds then build their nest inside the box.

113

Growing birds

All birds lay eggs. The parent birds look after the eggs to make sure the baby chicks hatch. Then they feed the baby birds until the chicks are big enough to leave the nest.

Keeping warm

Birds' eggs must be kept warm if the chicks are to hatch. The parents do this by sitting on top of the eggs. This is called incubation.

Nest imposters

Cuckoos do not build nests. Instead, they lay their eggs in the nests of other birds, who then look after the baby cuckoos. Baby cuckoos are bigger than the other chicks in the nest, so they get most of the food.

Baby birds

Newly hatched chicks are weak and parents must give them all the food they need. Sometimes, parents will swallow the food and then bring it back up for the chicks to eat.

DID YOU KNOW?

Ostriches lay the largest birds' eggs. Each egg is about 7 inches long and weighs 2 to 3 pounds.

Leaving the nest

As the chicks grow, the parents bring back more and more food. When the chicks are strong enough, they will try a few short practice flights. Then they will leave the nest for good.

This eagle chick is now ready to leave its nest.

Bat senses

Most bats hunt at night, when it is too dark to see. Instead of using their eyes, some bats use sounds to detect objects. This is called echolocation.

Large ears

Most bats have large ears, which gives them excellent hearing. They use their ears to collect sounds in the dark and to help them locate their prey.

Vampire bats cut the skin of their prey and lap up the blood.

Heat-seeking vampires

Vampires are blood-sucking bats. They feed on the blood of cows, pigs, horses, and birds. They detect their prey at night using special heat sensors in their faces.

Hearing in the dark

Echolocation is the use of sounds and echoes to find objects. Bats make very high-pitched sounds. These sounds hit an object and an echo comes back. A bat can tell where this object is, and how big it is, by listening to the echo.

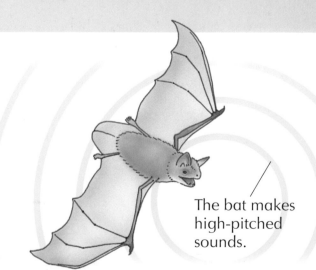

The bat makes high-pitched sounds.

DID YOU KNOW?

Vampire bats can drink about one-and-a-half times their body weight in blood in one feed. They need to eat at least two tablespoons of blood each day.

Fruit bats have larger eyes than other bats because they hunt during the day.

Large eyes

Fruit bats do not use echolocation. Instead, they have large eyes, which they use to find fruit in the rain forest. They also use their noses to smell their food.

The sounds bounce off the moth as echoes and travel back to the bat.

Flying insects

Most insects have two pairs of wings, which they use to fly. Insect wings vary in shape, from the thin wings of bees to the large, colorful wings of butterflies.

Hard to catch

Houseflies have only one pair of wings, but they are still among the fastest insects. They use their speed to escape attackers.

Insect hunters

Dragonflies have two pairs of long, see-through wings. These powerful insects are excellent fliers and can catch smaller insects in midair.

Dragonflies have large eyes for finding prey.

Buzzing bees

The honeybee has two pairs of very thin wings. It beats these wings so quickly that they make a buzzing sound. A bee can fly at 20 miles per hour.

DID YOU KNOW?

Most insects do not use their mouths to make sounds. Instead, they rub their wings or legs together to make a noise.

Colorful butterflies

Butterfly wings are covered in tiny scales. These scales can be a wide range of colors.

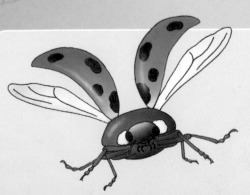

Ladybug wings

The ladybug has a pair of tough, red and black wings. These cover a second pair of wings, which are very delicate. The ladybug uses the second pair for flying.

Changing insects

Insects change a lot as they hatch from eggs and grow into adults. Some even change the entire shape of their bodies from long, thin caterpillars into winged moths and butterflies.

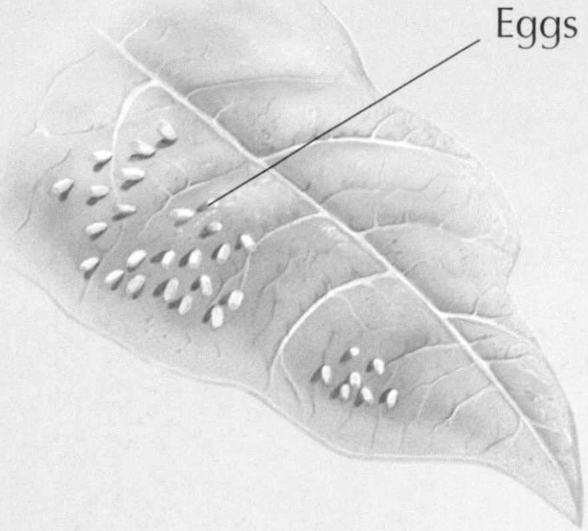

Eggs

Egg

A female butterfly lays tiny eggs on the leaves of plants.

Leaf muncher

The eggs hatch into young insects called larvae. The larvae of butterflies are known as caterpillars. Caterpillars eat leaves and grow very quickly.

Caterpillar

Butterfly

When the caterpillar has completely changed, the chrysalis splits open and a fully grown butterfly emerges. It spreads its wings so that they can dry. Then it flies away to eat and, if it is a female, to lay more eggs.

Adult butterfly

As a pupa, the caterpillar surrounds itself with a hard case called a chrysalis.

Hard case

When a caterpillar has reached full size, it turns into a pupa. This is the stage when the insect changes from a caterpillar into a butterfly. This change can take several weeks.

123

The desert locust

Desert locusts are a kind of grasshopper. Unlike most grasshoppers, desert locusts can cause huge amounts of damage by eating all the plants in a region.

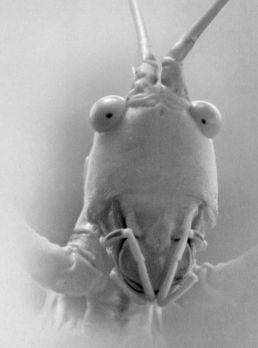

A locust's head

A locust has a pair of eyes, plus two feelers on top of its head called antennae. Its jaws have jagged edges to chew through leaves.

Swarms of locusts can fly up to 80 miles in a day.

Huge swarms

Sometimes, locusts join together in massive groups, called swarms. Some swarms are 25 miles long and contain billions of insects.

124

Flying and jumping

An adult locust has two pairs of wings. The front pair is hard and covers the rear pair of wings. Locusts also have a long pair of back legs that they use for jumping.

An adult locust can eat its own weight in food every day.

Locust facts

🐾 Locusts make a chirruping noise by rubbing their long back legs together.

🐾 A large swarm of locusts can eat up to 90,000 tons of food in a single day—that's the same weight as 10,000 African elephants.

Rear wings

Hidden wings

The hind, or rear, pair of wings on a locust is only seen when the insect is flying. With these wings, a locust can fly 12 miles per hour.

Living in water

Nearly three-quarters of the earth is covered by water. Water can be found almost everywhere, from enormous oceans to tiny streams. The oceans and seas are filled with saltwater. The water in streams, rivers, and lakes is called freshwater because it does not contain salt. Within these aquatic, or watery, worlds is a wide range of habitats, including coral reefs, swamps, and the deep, dark ocean.

How do fish swim?

Fish have powerful tails, which they move from side to side to push them through the water. They also have a number of fins on their bodies that they use to guide them.

Fast-swimming fish

The fastest fish in the ocean are sailfish and tuna. Their bodies are streamlined, or smooth and thin, so that they can slip through the water easily.

DID YOU KNOW?

The sailfish is the fastest fish. It can swim at speeds of up to 70 miles per hour. This is faster than the fastest land mammal, the cheetah, can run.

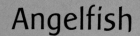
Tuna

Angelfish

Angelfish have a different body shape from tuna. Their bodies are squashed from side to side. This means that are not very fast swimmers, but they can twist and turn quickly.

Fish fins

A fish has a number of fins, each with a special job. The pectoral fins and the pelvic fins help with steering and stopping. The dorsal fin helps to keep the fish upright in the water.

Pectoral fin
Dorsal fin
Tail
Pelvic fin

126

Living in a group

Many types of fish swim together in large groups called schools. It is safer for fish to swim in schools because hunters can easily get confused by all the fish darting around.

A manta ray's wings can measure 23 feet across.

Flying underwater

A manta ray looks something like a huge airplane underwater. Its fins extend from its body to create enormous wings. The ray swims by flapping these wings to "fly" through the water.

129

Lakes and ponds

The water in ponds and lakes is called still water because it hardly moves. Animals living there do not have to swim against a flow of water as they do in streams and rivers.

Plant life

Plants, such as reeds, grow in the shallow water around the edges of lakes and ponds. Many animals like to hide among the plant stems and eat the leaves.

Newts

Newts belong to a group of animals called amphibians. They spend most of their time swimming in the water, but they also have legs so that they can walk across land.

This newt is brightly colored to warn other animals that it is poisonous.

Freshwater fish

Many different kinds of fish are found in ponds and lakes, including this cichlid. Some fish feed on plants, while others hunt and eat other animals.

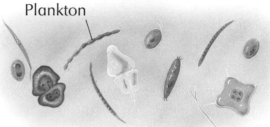

Plankton

Microscopic life

Pond water is full of tiny living things that are too small for us to see. These are called plankton, and they include small plants, larvae (baby insects), and fish eggs.

Dragonfly larvae spend the first year of their lives in the water hunting other animals.

Dragonfly larvae

Dragonflies lay their eggs in water. The young that hatch from the eggs are called larvae. When the larvae become adults, they leave the water and fly away.

131

The salmon

Salmon spend the first part of their lives in rivers. Then they travel to the sea, where they live for the next few years eating fish and shellfish. After this, they make a long journey back to the river where they were born.

Powerful fish

Salmon are large, powerful fish. Their bodies are long and slim, which is ideal for swimming, and they have strong muscles to push them through the water.

Salmon swim by flicking their tails from side to side.

Salmon facts

- Salmon live in both the Atlantic and Pacific oceans.
- The main types of salmon are the Atlantic, sockeye, chinook, pink, chum, coho, and cherry salmon.
- Sockeye salmon may swim more than 900 miles from the Pacific Ocean to the rivers where they lay their eggs.

With a powerful flick of its tail, a salmon jumps up a waterfall.

A feast of salmon

As the salmon swim up rivers and streams, other animals hunt them. Grizzly bears wait in the shallow parts of the rivers and use their strong jaws to catch the salmon as they swim past.

Heading up the river

Salmon spend most of their lives in the ocean. However, they have to lay their eggs in streams. Every year, millions of adult salmon swim into rivers, against the flow of the water. The journey is long and tiring and the salmon have to get over many obstacles, including waterfalls.

Farming salmon

People build special farms where they raise salmon to eat. The fish are kept in large floating cages, like the ones above, for up to 18 months.

133

Frogs and toads

Frogs and toads belong to a group of animals called amphibians, which lay their eggs in water. Tadpoles hatch out of these eggs and change their shape as they grow into adults.

Frog spawn

A female frog lays about 100 eggs, which stick together in a clump called frog spawn. Each egg contains a tiny black dot that grows into a tadpole.

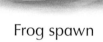

Frog spawn

Toads

Toads look very much like frogs, but there are a few differences. For example, toads usually have skin with warts, while a frog's skin is smooth.

Adult frogs

The froglets grow into adult frogs. Adults have large eyes and wide mouths, plus powerful back legs.

Froglet

Froglets

The tadpoles then grow front legs and their tails start to shrink. They are now called froglets, and they are ready to leave the water.

Tadpole with legs

Tadpoles

Young tadpoles

Tadpoles have long tails but no legs. They breathe using gills, just like a fish.

Growing legs

The tadpoles grow larger very quickly. About eight weeks after hatching, they have grown back legs.

Rivers

Animals that live in rivers have to cope with flowing water. Rivers also carry small pieces of mud and stones, which can make it difficult to see underwater.

River life

The mud on a riverbed is very good for plants to grow. The plants attract insects and other small animals to the rivers. These small creatures attract larger animals, such as fish and birds.

Female trout dig small nests in the gravel on riverbeds where they lay their eggs.

Trout

The trout is a type of fish that loves fast-flowing water in streams and rivers. Its skin is brown and spotted, which helps it to hide among the mud and stones of a riverbed.

136

A dragonfly's huge eyes let the insect see all around its body.

River insects

Dragonflies are active hunters along river banks, catching insects while in flight. Other insects that live near rivers include damselflies and mayflies, which lay their eggs in the water.

DID YOU KNOW?

Electric eels live in the rivers of South America. They produce enough electricity to power 12 lightbulbs. They use this electricity to stun prey.

River birds

Swans and ducks are common along rivers, eating plants that grow on river banks or in the water. Swans build large nests on the river bank to raise their young, which are called cygnets.

Black swans live in southern Australia.

Estuaries

Estuaries are places where rivers flow into the sea. They are large, flat areas with a lot of mud that small animals can burrow into.

The Nile Delta forms where the river meets the Mediterranean.

River Nile

River deltas

When a river reaches an estuary, it slows down and drops the mud it was carrying. This mud builds up to form a large, triangle-shaped area called a delta.

Cormorants can dive down to depths of 150 feet.

DID YOU KNOW?

Some kinds of shore crab can run at up to 10 miles per hour.

Fish divers

Cormorants live alongside rivers, lakes, estuaries, and seashores. They dive into the water to catch fish to eat. Some cormorants have even been trained to catch fish for humans.

138

Ragworms

A ragworm digs a U-shaped burrow into the mud. It then shoots its long jaws out of this burrow to catch and eat any small animal that gets too near.

Ragworms have flat bodies covered in bristles.

Beach hunters

Shore crabs are found on the mud of estuaries, the seashore, and small streams. They eat other animals that live in the mud, such as worms.

Shore crabs burrow into the mud to escape from birds.

Cockles

Cockles are bivalves. This means that they have two shells that are joined together. They dig into the mud when the tide is out, then they come out to eat when the tide comes in and they are covered by water.

Wading birds

Estuaries attract large flocks, or groups, of birds. This is because the mud is full of small animals that birds love to eat. Each kind of bird has a different shape of beak for catching different animals.

Curlews

Curlews have long, curved beaks. They push their beaks into the mud to find worms, shrimp, and crabs.

Long legs

Many of the birds found in estuaries, such as flamingoes, have very long legs. They use these long legs to wade, or walk, through the water, looking for food.

140

Spearing fish

The heron has a long, pointed beak. It stands in the water and does not move. Once it sees a fish, it darts its head quickly forward and catches the fish in its beak.

Oystercatchers

The oystercatcher has a strong, orange-red beak. It uses this to force open the closed shells of cockles and mussels to reach the animals inside.

Herons stand with their necks bent into an S shape.

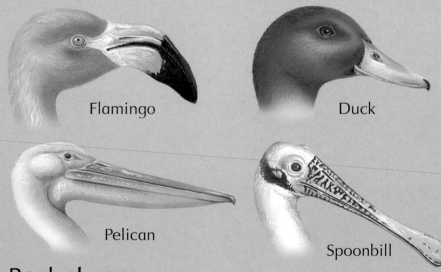

Flamingo

Duck

Pelican

Spoonbill

Beak shapes

Flamingoes use their bent beaks to strain tiny animals out of the water. Ducks have a flat beak that can strain animals out of the mud. Pelicans have large pouches under their beaks, which they use to catch fish. Spoonbills have spoon-shaped beaks for scooping up animals from the mud.

141

Sandy beaches

Sandy beaches may look deserted, especially when the tide is out. But there are a lot of animals hiding beneath the sand.

Looking empty

When the tide goes out, beach animals dig into the sand to hide from the sun, wind, and any hunters. They come out of hiding when the tide comes back in.

Worms leave small piles of sand, called worm casts, at the entrances to their burrows.

Cockles

Mussel

Spider crab

Thin telin

Sand gaper

Lugworm

146

forests

...type of giant seaweed that ...underwater forests. These ...nd in shallow water near ...shore. The huge seaweed ...provide shelter for fish and ...sea creatures.

Inside the forest

Giant kelp can grow to 200 feet in length. It attaches itself to the seabed by roots called holdfasts. Thousands of fish swim between these massive blades of kelp, hiding from hunters, such as sharks.

...nge garibaldis

...bright orange color ...he garibaldi fish is a ...rning to other fish in ...e forest to stay away. ...aribaldis are very ...ggressive fish and will ...ven attack human divers!

Kelp

Kelp is a
grows in
are fou
the se
forest
other

Org

The
of t
w
th

Razorshell

Sea otters sometimes use rocks to smash open any shellfish.

Sea otters

Sea otters swim through the kelp looking for sea urchins to eat. They even sleep in the kelp forests, wrapping themselves up in kelp leaves so they do not float away.

Eagle rays

Eagle rays have an excellent sense of smell. They like to sniff out mussels and other shellfish, which they crunch up using their strong teeth.

The large wings on an eagle ray can measure more than 6 feet across.

DID YOU KNOW?

Giant kelp is one of the fastest growing plants in the world. When conditions are good, kelp can grow more than 18 inches in a day!

149

Mangrove swamps

Mangrove swamps are found along coasts near the Equator, which runs around the middle of the world. The water in these swamps is a mixture of saltwater and freshwater. It is called brackish water.

Mangrove trees

The mangrove is an odd-looking tree. Its tangled roots act like stilts, holding the tree above the water.

Fiddler crabs are small, measuring just under 1 inch across.

Waving claws

Male fiddler crabs have one claw that is much larger than the other. They use these huge claws to wave at and attract females.

150

Wading birds

Egrets wade through the swamp water on their long legs, using their feet to stir up mud on the bottom. This mud attracts small fish, frogs, and insects, which the egrets catch and eat.

Land fish

The mudskipper is a type of fish that can move over land as well as through water. It "walks" using its pectoral fins like little legs.

When the tide goes out, mudskippers move over land from pool to pool.

DID YOU KNOW?

The Sundarbans in Bangladesh and India is the largest mangrove swamp in the world. It lies where the Ganges River flows into the Indian Ocean.

Coral reefs

Coral reefs are some of the richest habitats in the world. They are home to millions of different creatures, including hunting sharks and enormous shellfish.

Skeleton home

Coral reefs are made by tiny creatures called coral polyps. Some of the polyps have a hard outer covering called a skeleton. When the polyps die, the skeletons are left behind and gradually build up to form the reef.

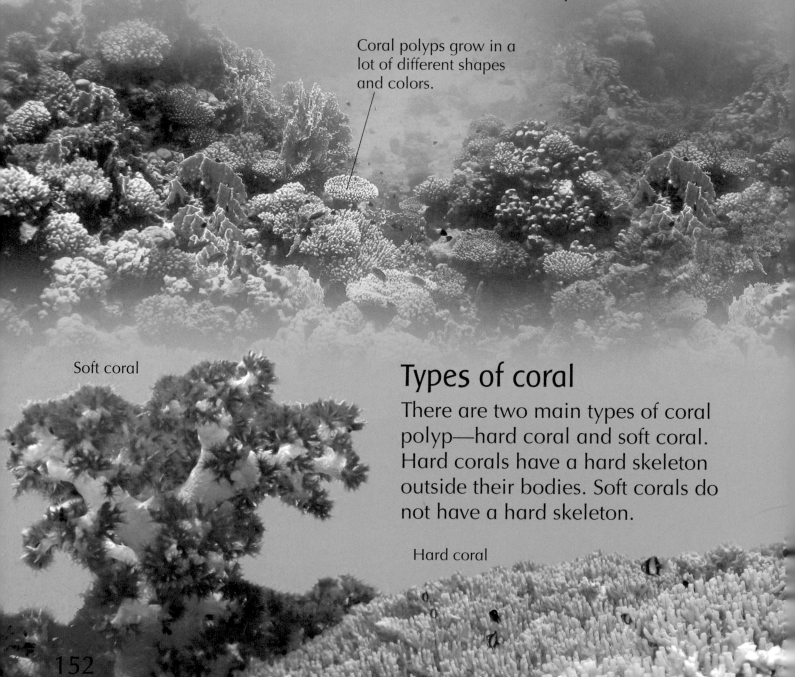

Coral polyps grow in a lot of different shapes and colors.

Soft coral

Types of coral

There are two main types of coral polyp—hard coral and soft coral. Hard corals have a hard skeleton outside their bodies. Soft corals do not have a hard skeleton.

Hard coral

Reef hunters

Reef sharks are among the largest hunters on the reef. Some sharks swim in groups, called packs, looking for small fish to eat.

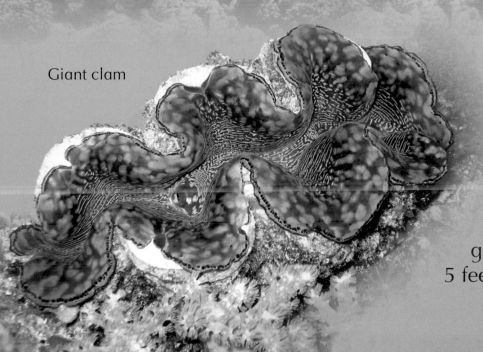

Giant clam

Giant clams

Giant clams are bivalves, meaning they have two shells that are joined together. These huge shellfish can grow to more than 5 feet across.

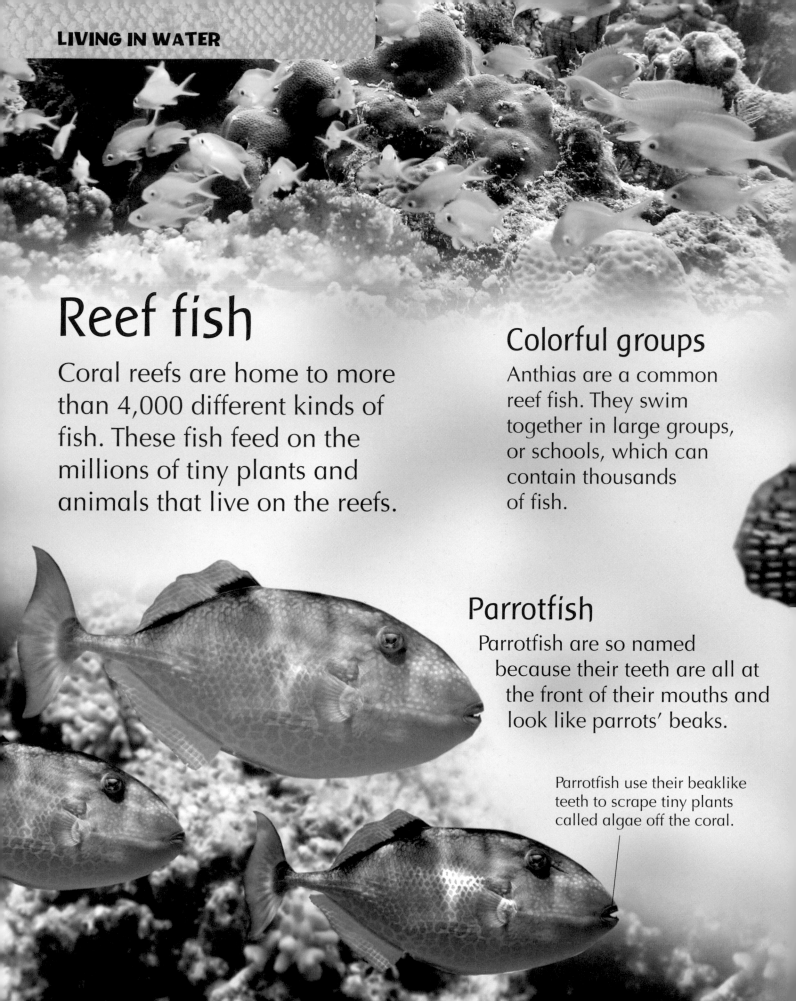

Reef fish

Coral reefs are home to more than 4,000 different kinds of fish. These fish feed on the millions of tiny plants and animals that live on the reefs.

Colorful groups

Anthias are a common reef fish. They swim together in large groups, or schools, which can contain thousands of fish.

Parrotfish

Parrotfish are so named because their teeth are all at the front of their mouths and look like parrots' beaks.

Parrotfish use their beaklike teeth to scrape tiny plants called algae off the coral.

Beautiful but dangerous

The brightly colored stripes of the lionfish are a warning that this is a dangerous creature. The fish's long spines contain a poison that can kill other animals.

Living together

Anemones have stinging cells in their tentacles, which can hurt most fish. But clownfish can live among the tentacles because they are covered in a slime that protects them from the stings.

155

Open ocean

The vast areas of open water between islands and continents are full of fish, whales, squid, and other animals. Most of these animals are found near the water's surface, where there is plenty of sunlight.

A whale shark's mouth is 5 feet wide.

Huge but harmless

The whale shark is a huge fish. It swims near the ocean's surface, using its enormous mouth to strain tiny animals from the sea water.

DID YOU KNOW?

Whale sharks are the largest fish swimming in the oceans. They often grow to more than 30 feet long.

Whales are mammals and need to come to the water's surface to breathe.

Giant whales

The largest animals in the oceans are the whales. This is a beluga whale. Even though belugas are one of the smallest whales, they can still grow to 13 feet long.

Cuttlefish

Cuttlefish belong to a group of animals called mollusks. They have eight short tentacles and two long tentacles that are covered in suckers.

Cuttlefish use their tentacles to pull food into their mouths.

Sea turtles

Green turtles are found in the warm waters of the Atlantic, Pacific, and Indian Oceans. They feed mainly on sea grasses and small plants called algae.

Microscopic life

Tiny animals called plankton float near the surface of the ocean. These animals are eaten by larger creatures, such as krill and fish. The krill and fish are themselves eaten by even larger animals, such as whales and dolphins. Without plankton, none of these animals would survive.

When they are large enough, crab larvae sink to the seabed and grow into adult crabs.

Young sea creatures

Plankton contains the larvae, or young, of many animals, including crabs. Crabs live on the seabed but their larvae float about in the water.

The bodies of baby fish are almost see-through, to hide them in the water.

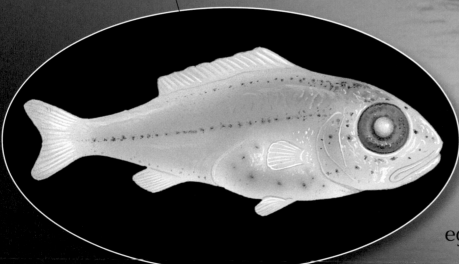

Baby fish

Plankton also contains many types of young fish including herring, eels, and cod. These young fish hatch from eggs laid by adult fish.

Krill

Krill are pink, shrimplike animals that are up to 6 inches long. They gather together in large groups called swarms. These swarms can be so big that they turn the water pink.

Some whales have baleen plates that are more than 16 feet long.

Plankton feeders

Many large whales eat krill and plankton. They swallow water and strain out the animals using long, bony plates, called baleen plates, in their mouths.

DID YOU KNOW? Female krill can lay up to 10,000 eggs at a time, several times a year.

159

Ocean hunters

The ocean is not a safe place for a small animal because there are a lot of hunters looking for their next meal. These hunters include birds flying above the surface, large fish such as barracudas, and mammals such as whales.

Schools of herring

The herring is a type of fish that lives in large schools, or groups. Ocean hunters are attracted to these schools because there are plenty of fish to eat.

Fast-swimming hunters

Barracudas are fast-swimming hunting fish that can grow to nearly 6 feet long. They swim in large groups, looking for other fish to attack.

Barracudas can swim at more than 25 miles per hour.

Dive bombers

Pelicans fly over the ocean waiting for fish to swim near the surface. Then they dive into the water and scoop up fish in the pouches under their beaks.

Sensitive sharks

Sharks have very good senses to detect prey. They can smell a tiny drop of blood and can feel the twitches made by an injured fish from very far away.

DID YOU KNOW?

Sharks have been living in the oceans for more than 400 million years.

Whales

Whales belong to a group of animals called mammals. They have to breathe air, just like humans. They do this through a nostril on top of the head, called a blowhole.

Breaching

Scientists do not know why whales leap out of the water in a move called breaching. It may be to attract a partner or to knock off other animals that are stuck to their bodies.

Like all mammals, baby whales feed on milk made by their mothers.

Baby whales

Instead of laying eggs, whales give birth to live babies. As soon as a baby whale is born, its mother pushes it to the surface to take its first breath of air.

Whale facts

🐾 There are two main kinds of whale: toothed whales, which have teeth, and baleen whales, which have baleen plates instead of teeth for straining food from water.

🐾 A baby blue whale will drink up to 200 quarts of milk from its mother every day—that is as much as 600 cans of soda.

Killer whales

Killer whales, or orcas, live together in groups of up to 40 members. They hunt together as a group, looking for fish, birds, squid, and even other whales to eat.

Dolphins

Dolphins are small whales. They have snouts that look like a beak. These snouts are filled with small teeth that are used to catch fish.

Dolphins live in small groups called pods.

DID YOU KNOW?

The world's biggest animal is the blue whale. It can grow to about 100 feet long.

Life on the seabed

The seabed is covered with a thick layer of slimy mud and the remains of dead animals. Most of the animals that live here will eat these dead remains. This is called scavenging.

The water is heated by red-hot rocks just beneath the seabed.

Hot-water animals

In some of the deepest oceans, hot water escapes through chimneys in the seabed. Many animals live near these chimneys, such as giant tube worms and mussels.

Mussels

Tube worms

DID YOU KNOW? The largest crab in the world is the Japanese spider crab. It can grow to 12 feet across—that is more than twice the size of two adult humans.

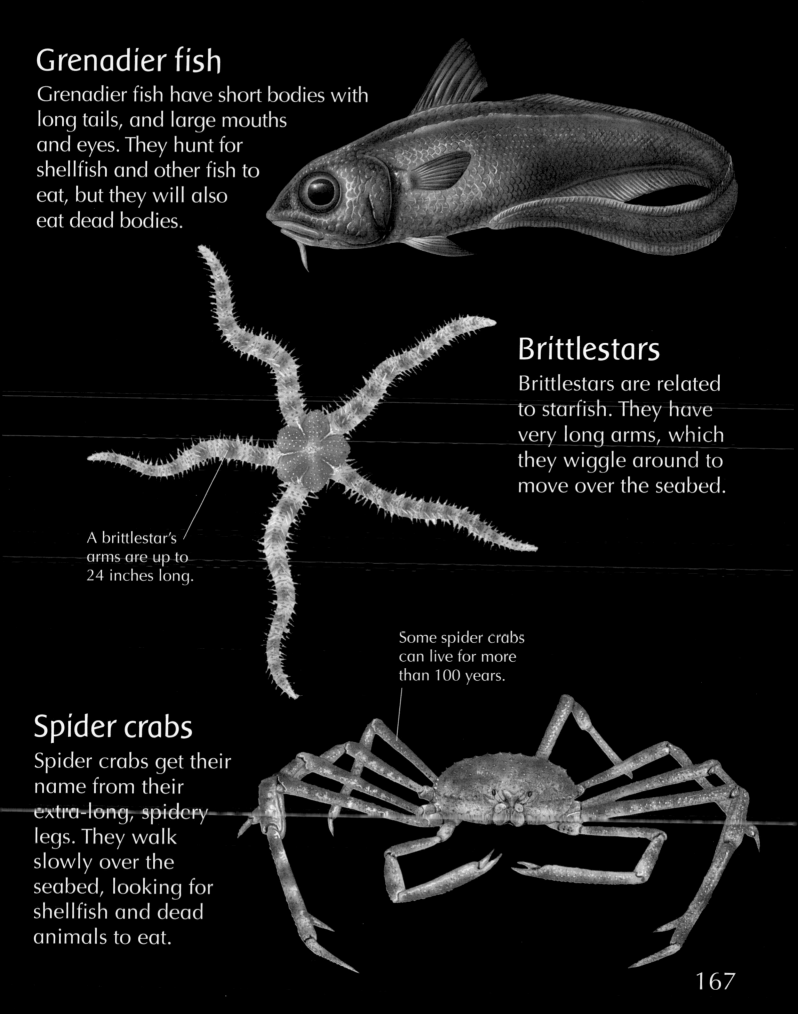

Grenadier fish

Grenadier fish have short bodies with
long tails, and large mouths
and eyes. They hunt for
shellfish and other fish to
eat, but they will also
eat dead bodies.

Brittlestars

Brittlestars are related
to starfish. They have
very long arms, which
they wiggle around to
move over the seabed.

A brittlestar's
arms are up to
24 inches long.

Some spider crabs
can live for more
than 100 years.

Spider crabs

Spider crabs get their
name from their
extra-long, spidery
legs. They walk
slowly over the
seabed, looking for
shellfish and dead
animals to eat.

Saving our wildlife

We call an animal "endangered" when very few individuals are alive. For example, the tiger is endangered because only a few thousand are left in the wild. An animal becomes extinct when the last one dies. Sadly, many thousands of different species, or kinds, of animal are endangered, and hundreds become extinct every year.

Conserving animals

The best way to save endangered animals is to conserve, or protect, their habitats. This can be done by creating national parks and by stopping farms and factories from polluting the land.

Watching animals

Some African countries, such as South Africa and Tanzania, have turned large areas into game reserves and national parks. Animals that live inside these areas are protected from pollution and human hunters.

Bird watching

People can watch animals in protected areas. This building is called a hide, and people use it to watch birds without disturbing them.

Many tourists visit game reserves and national parks to watch the animals.

DID YOU KNOW? The U.S.'s Yellowstone National Park was the world's first national park. It was created in 1872.

Cleaning up

Everybody can help to protect animal habitats. Garbage can be harmful to animals, so these people are cleaning it out of a pond.

Organic farming

Many farmers use chemicals called pesticides and fertilizers to grow their crops. These chemicals can harm wildlife. Organic farming is a way of farming that does not use these chemicals, so wild animals are not harmed.

These pigs on an organic farm are free range, which means they are allowed to walk outside.

Back from the brink

Some animals have been saved from extinction. This has happened because people have stopped killing them and zoos have bred them to increase their numbers.

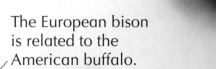

The European bison is related to the American buffalo.

Hunted for fur

Northern fur seals were hunted for their fur and were almost extinct by the early 1900s. In 1911, the people killing the seals agreed to stop hunting them. Since then, the number of fur seals has increased.

European bison

Because of hunting, the European bison, or wisent, disappeared from the wild in 1927. But 50 bison still lived in zoos, and these produced young. Bison have now been released back into forests in Poland and Russia.

The ne-ne

The ne-ne, or Hawaiian goose, is found only on the Hawaiian Islands. In 1949, there were fewer than 30 left. Some of these were caught and taken to breeding centers around the world. Now, more than 1,000 birds live in the wild.

DID YOU KNOW?

The Takahe is a flightless bird that lives in New Zealand. People thought it was extinct in 1898, but it was rediscovered 50 years later.

Golden lion tamarins

Fewer than 100 golden lion tamarins survived in the forests of Brazil by 1984. Luckily, more of these monkeys have been bred in zoos and released back into the wild.

All kinds of animals

To make it easy to identify and name the millions of creatures there are in the world, scientists group animals together according to their structure. So, for example, animals with six legs belong to a group called insects, and those with feathers belong to another group called birds. By studying an animal's features, we can work out what group it belongs to.

177

Grouping animals

All animals belong to a group called the animal kingdom. This is divided into two groups, which are divided again and again into ever-smaller groups. An individual animal, such as the polar bear, is known as a species.

Polar bears belong to a group of animals called mammals.

With or without backbones

Animals divide into two groups: those without backbones, called invertebrates, and those with backbones—vertebrates. These are split into smaller groups, for example, vertebrates divide into fish, amphibians, reptiles, birds, and mammals.

What is a polar bear?

- It belongs to the animal kingdom
- It is a vertebrate (has a backbone)
- It is a mammal (mothers make milk)
- It is a bear (a kind of mammal)
- It is a polar bear (its common name)

178

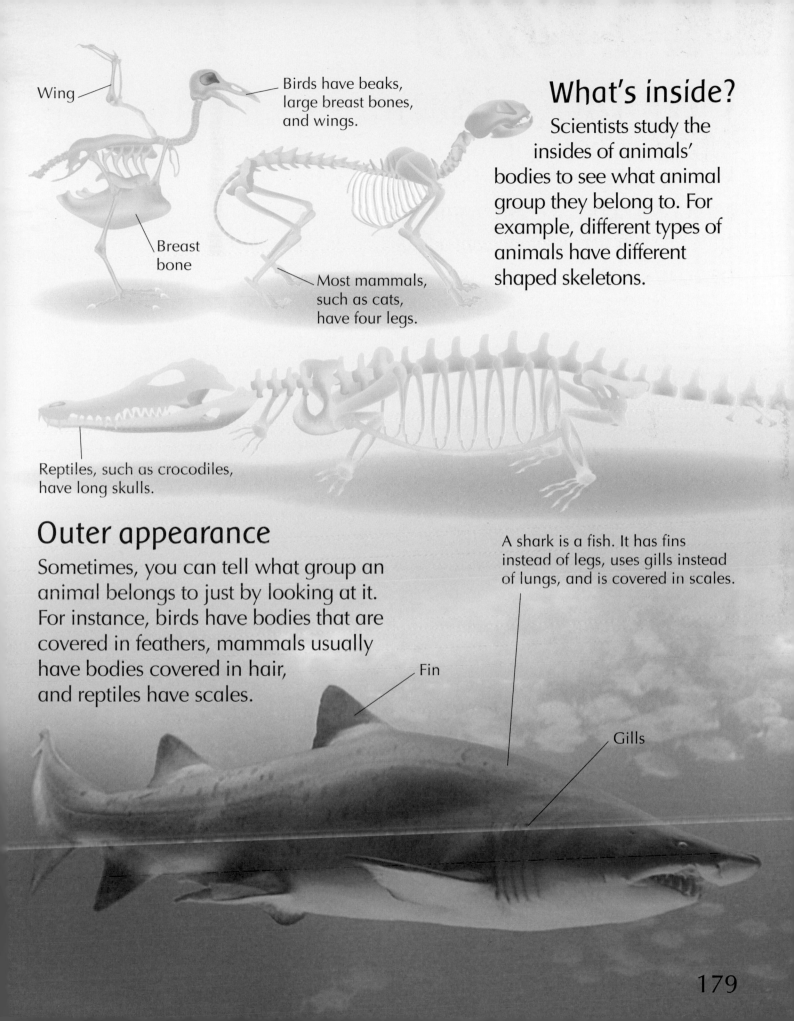

Wing

Birds have beaks, large breast bones, and wings.

Breast bone

Most mammals, such as cats, have four legs.

What's inside?

Scientists study the insides of animals' bodies to see what animal group they belong to. For example, different types of animals have different shaped skeletons.

Reptiles, such as crocodiles, have long skulls.

Outer appearance

Sometimes, you can tell what group an animal belongs to just by looking at it. For instance, birds have bodies that are covered in feathers, mammals usually have bodies covered in hair, and reptiles have scales.

A shark is a fish. It has fins instead of legs, uses gills instead of lungs, and is covered in scales.

Fin

Gills

179

Anemones

🐾 Anemones have rings of arms, called tentacles, around their mouths.

🐾 These tentacles can sting other animals. Anemones use their stinging tentacles to catch their food and pull it into their mouths.

Sponges, anemones, and jellyfish

Sponges, anemones, and jellyfish are invertebrates, or animals without backbones. They live in water and have a tube-shaped body that is open at one end.

Mouth

Tentacles

These are tube sponges. They can be 3 feet long.

Sponges

🐾 Sponges cannot move and remain attached to the seabed.

🐾 They eat by drawing water through holes in their bodies and filtering out tiny plants and animals. floating in it to eat.

Jellyfish

- Jellyfish have bell-shaped bodies at the top with a lot of stinging tentacles hanging below.

- They eat small animals and plants that they catch in their tentacles.

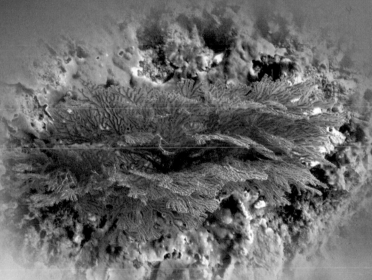

Fan corals

- Fan corals are made up of millions of tiny creatures called polyps. Polyps look a little like tiny anemones.

- Fan corals are found in warm seas and can grow to nearly 10 feet in size.

Staghorn coral gets its name because it looks like the antlers of a stag.

Hard corals

- Hard corals have tough skeletons that are left behind after the animals die. These skeletons build up over many years to form coral reefs.

- Staghorn corals can grow up to 8 inches every year.

Worms

Worms are animals without backbones. Many live in water, while others live underground. Some worms live inside the bodies of animals and are called parasites.

Earthworms

- Earthworms are a kind of segmented worm. Their bodies are split into sections called segments.

- Earthworms eat dead and rotting leaves, which they pull down into the tunnels they dig through the soil.

Tapeworms use these sharp hooks to dig into the guts of animals.

Tapeworms

- Tapeworms are parasites that live in the guts of other animals. They eat the other animals' food.

- Some kinds of tapeworm can grow to 50 feet in length.

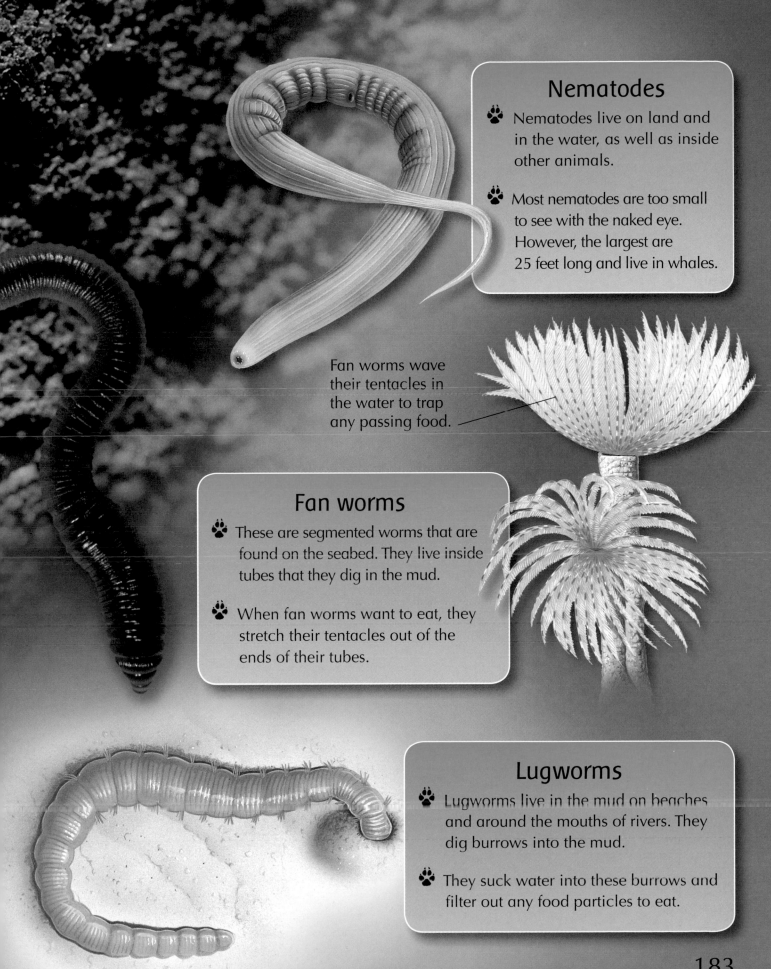

Nematodes

- Nematodes live on land and in the water, as well as inside other animals.

- Most nematodes are too small to see with the naked eye. However, the largest are 25 feet long and live in whales.

Fan worms wave their tentacles in the water to trap any passing food.

Fan worms

- These are segmented worms that are found on the seabed. They live inside tubes that they dig in the mud.

- When fan worms want to eat, they stretch their tentacles out of the ends of their tubes.

Lugworms

- Lugworms live in the mud on beaches and around the mouths of rivers. They dig burrows into the mud.

- They suck water into these burrows and filter out any food particles to eat.

Insects

Insects belong to a very large group of creatures called arthropods. Adult insects have three body parts: a head, a middle section called the thorax, and a tail section called the abdomen. They all have six legs.

Fleas

🐾 Fleas are tiny insects that are parasites. This means that they live on and feed from other animals.

🐾 Fleas have powerful back legs and can jump 150 times their body length.

This swallowtail butterfly has a fork-shaped tail, just like a swallow.

Butterflies

🐾 There are 17,500 different species, or kinds, of butterfly.

🐾 Butterflies have two pairs of wings. Each pair is joined together by tiny hooks, so that they flap at the same time.

Cockroaches

 Cockroaches are some of the oldest insects on the earth. They have been around for 320 million years.

 Cockroaches have long, flattened bodies that are covered in tough external, or outer, skeletons.

Eye

Dragonflies keep their wings open when resting.

Dragonflies

 Dragonflies have two pairs of wings that are usually see-through. Many have long, thin abdomens.

 Dragonflies have huge eyes, which let them see right around their bodies.

Abdomen   Thorax   Head

Ants

 An ant has a large head and a long, oval-shaped abdomen that is joined to the thorax by a thin waist.

 Most kinds of ant live together in huge groups called colonies.

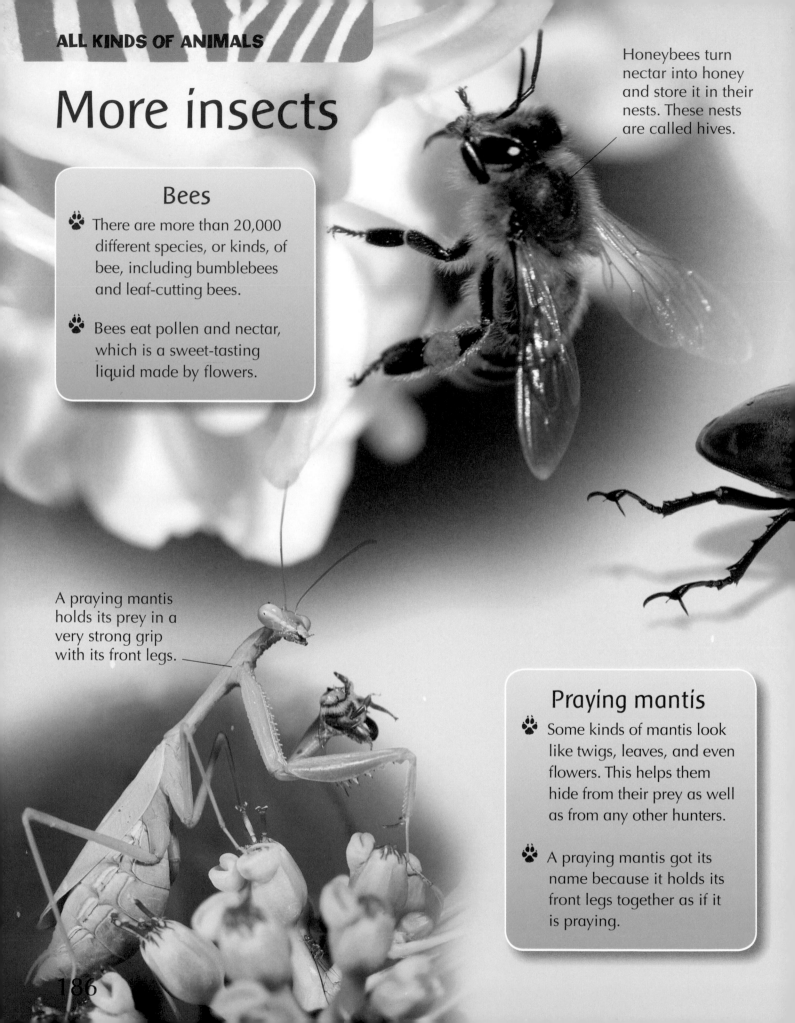

More insects

Honeybees turn nectar into honey and store it in their nests. These nests are called hives.

Bees

🐾 There are more than 20,000 different species, or kinds, of bee, including bumblebees and leaf-cutting bees.

🐾 Bees eat pollen and nectar, which is a sweet-tasting liquid made by flowers.

A praying mantis holds its prey in a very strong grip with its front legs.

Praying mantis

🐾 Some kinds of mantis look like twigs, leaves, and even flowers. This helps them hide from their prey as well as from any other hunters.

🐾 A praying mantis got its name because it holds its front legs together as if it is praying.

186

Ladybugs

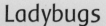 Ladybugs have bright red, yellow, or black markings. They are a kind of insect called a beetle.

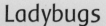 Ladybugs are important to gardeners and farmers because they eat aphids. Aphids are tiny insects that cause a lot of damage to plants.

Ladybugs are poisonous to birds and small lizards.

Stag beetle

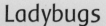 Stag beetles got their name because of their huge jaws, which look like the antlers of a stag.

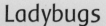 These jaws are so big that they can make up half of a stag beetle's total length.

Stag beetles use their huge jaws to wrestle with each other.

A wasp's yellow and black bands warn other animals about its sting.

Wasps

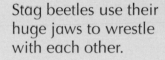 Many kinds of wasp live together in large nests. A few species live on their own, such as spider wasps.

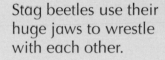 Wasps' nests are made from paper which the wasps make by chewing wood.

187

Crustaceans

A crustacean has a body that is covered with a tough shell called an external skeleton. Most crustaceans live in the water, but a few can survive on land.

Crabs

- Crabs live in the sea, on land, and in rivers. Their bodies are protected by thick shells called carapaces.

- The front legs on crabs have developed into large pinching claws which the crabs use to hold objects and prey.

Shrimp

- There are about 2,000 kinds of shrimp. Their long thin bodies are covered in a see-through shell.

- All shrimp swim backward by twitching their bodies and tails.

188

Wood lice

- These crustaceans live on land, usually in dark and damp places, where they eat rotting wood.

- Some wood lice roll up into tight balls for protection.

Water flea

- Water fleas, such as daphnia, are found in the freshwater of lakes and rivers, but a few live in the sea.

- Most water fleas are usually too small to see with the naked eye. However, some are as large as half an inch long.

Daphnia wave their antennae, or feelers, to move through the water.

Lobsters

- Lobsters have five pairs of legs. One or more of these pairs ends in pincers called chelae.

- Lobsters can either walk along the seabed or swim through the water by flicking their long tails.

189

Centipedes and millipedes

Millipedes and centipedes have long bodies that are split into many segments, or sections. Millipedes have two pairs of legs per segment, while centipedes have one pair of legs on each segment.

Centipedes

🐾 There are more than 5,000 different kinds of centipede. They usually live in woodlands, among the fallen leaves, except for house centipedes that can spend their entire lives inside buildings.

🐾 All centipedes are poisonous and use their poison to kill their prey.

House centipedes have very long legs that let them run quickly.

Giant centipedes

🐾 These are the largest kind of centipede. Some can grow to 12 inches long.

🐾 They are hunting centipedes. They come out at night and search for their prey, which can include vertebrate animals, such as mice.

190

Millipedes

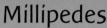 Unlike centipedes, millipedes are not hunters. Instead, they eat plants.

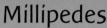 To protect themselves, millipedes roll up into tight coils. Some kinds of millipede give off a foul-smelling liquid that scares off any hunters.

Pill millipedes

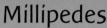 Pill millipedes are much shorter than other millipedes and are often mistaken for wood lice.

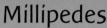 When threatened, they can roll up into balls to protect themselves.

Giant millipedes

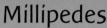 Giant millipedes can grow to a length of nearly 16 inches and are as thick as your thumb.

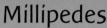 The largest millipedes have more than 100 segments to their bodies.

Some kinds of millipede can jump over an inch when they are attacked.

191

Arachnids

This group of animals includes spiders, scorpions, mites, and ticks. Arachnids have eight legs and, unlike insects, they only have two body parts: a head-thorax and a separate abdomen.

Web-weaving spiders

- Many kinds of spider produce thin threads of silk. Some weave the silk into sticky webs which they use to trap prey.

- Some spiders eat their webs at the end of each day when the stickiness has worn off. They then build fresh webs.

Orb-weaving spiders wrap their prey up in spider silk before feeding.

The black widow spider has one of the most powerful poisons in the world.

Poisonous spiders

- These spiders use poison to harm or kill other animals. The bite of about 200 kinds of spider can cause pain to a human or even death.

- A spider can choose whether or not to inject poison when it bites.

Hunting spiders

- These spiders do not build webs. Instead, they chase after prey or ambush unsuspecting animals.

- Hunting spiders include wolf spiders, tarantulas, and huntsman spiders.

Some female ticks can suck up 100 times their body weight in blood.

Ticks and mites

- Ticks and mites are parasites that live on and feed off other animals. They use their jaws to suck the other animals' blood.

- Some ticks and mites will rest on top of long blades of grass, waiting to jump onto passing animals.

Scorpions

- A scorpion has four pairs of legs. The front pair ends in pincers.

- The scorpion's tail curves over its body and ends in a sting that is used to paralyze prey.

183

Mollusks

Mollusks are invertebrates, which means they do not have backbones. They either have shells around the outside of their bodies or the remains of shells inside their bodies.

Cuttlefish can change color to hide from hunters.

Cuttlefish

🐾 Cuttlefish are related to octopuses and squid. They have shells inside their bodies.

🐾 Cuttlefish have eight short tentacles and two long ones, which they use to catch prey. They swim backward by forcing water out of their bodies in powerful jets.

Clams

🐾 Clams are bivalves. This means that they have two shells that are hinged so that they can open and close.

🐾 Giant clams can be more than 3 feet long and weigh nearly 450 pounds.

Limpets

🐾 These mollusks are covered with cone-shaped shells and live on rocks along the seashore.

🐾 Limpets move slowly over the rocks, eating tiny plants called algae. When the tide goes out, limpets pull their shells down tight and stick to the rocks.

Sea slugs

🐾 Many sea slugs are brightly colored. This warns other animals that they are poisonous.

🐾 Sea slugs eat other animals, including sponges and, sometimes, other sea slugs.

A snail moves about by stretching out its large foot.

Snails

🐾 Snails have coil-shaped shells and are found living on land as well as in rivers, lakes, and the sea.

🐾 When threatened, a snail will retreat into its shell and close a plate, called an operculum, over the opening.

195

Starfish, urchins, and cucumbers

These creatures belong to the group of animals called echinoderms. They are found in the sea, where they live on the shore, seabed, and coral reefs. Echinoderms do not have eyes, brains, or hearts.

Starfish can regrow any arms that they lose.

Sea cucumbers

🐾 These sluglike creatures have leathery or spiky skin and grow to a length of 7 feet.

🐾 Some kinds of sea cucumber throw out sticky threads when attacked, in order to confuse any hunters.

Starfish

🐾 There are more than 1,800 different kinds of starfish. They usually have five arms that are attached to a central body.

🐾 Some kinds of starfish have as many as 50 arms.

196

Sunstars

- Sunstars are a kind of starfish. They have between 8 and 16 arms and can measure 14 inches across.

- They crawl over the seabed hunting for shellfish and other starfish to eat.

Sea urchins

- Sea urchins are ball-shaped animals that are covered in spines.

- They hide in cracks between rocks. Their spines make it difficult for hunters to catch them and pull them out.

Sand dollars

- Sand dollars are a kind of urchin, with a flat body shaped like a coin.

- They live on beaches and burrow into the sand when the tide goes out.

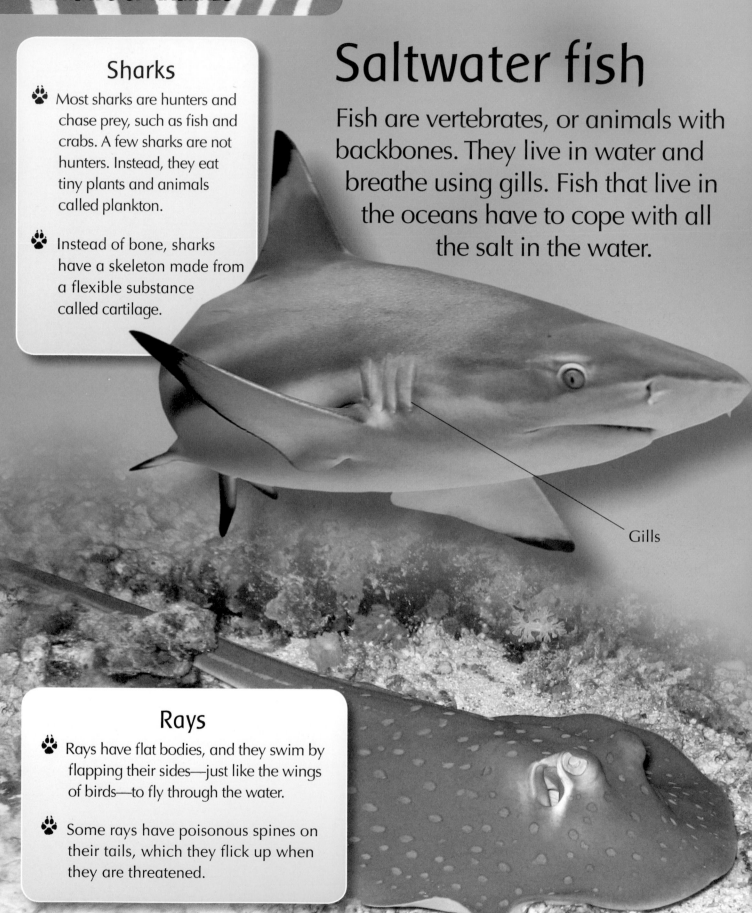

Sharks

- Most sharks are hunters and chase prey, such as fish and crabs. A few sharks are not hunters. Instead, they eat tiny plants and animals called plankton.

- Instead of bone, sharks have a skeleton made from a flexible substance called cartilage.

Saltwater fish

Fish are vertebrates, or animals with backbones. They live in water and breathe using gills. Fish that live in the oceans have to cope with all the salt in the water.

Gills

Rays

- Rays have flat bodies, and they swim by flapping their sides—just like the wings of birds—to fly through the water.

- Some rays have poisonous spines on their tails, which they flick up when they are threatened.

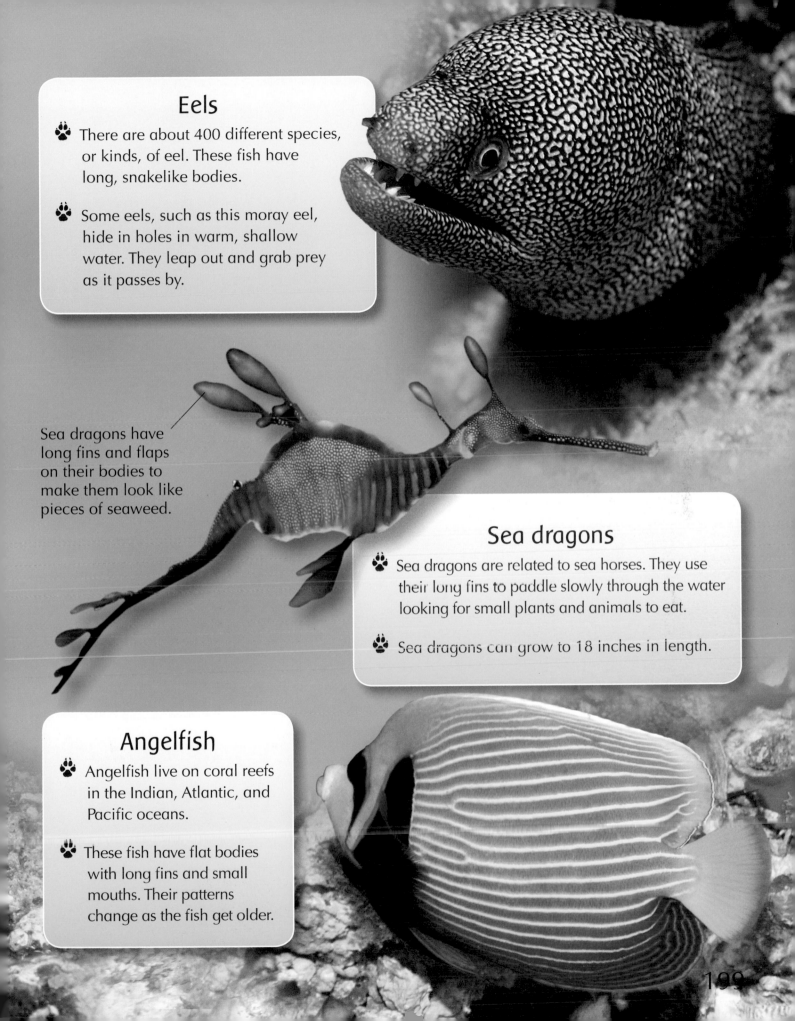

Eels

- There are about 400 different species, or kinds, of eel. These fish have long, snakelike bodies.

- Some eels, such as this moray eel, hide in holes in warm, shallow water. They leap out and grab prey as it passes by.

Sea dragons have long fins and flaps on their bodies to make them look like pieces of seaweed.

Sea dragons

- Sea dragons are related to sea horses. They use their long fins to paddle slowly through the water looking for small plants and animals to eat.

- Sea dragons can grow to 18 inches in length.

Angelfish

- Angelfish live on coral reefs in the Indian, Atlantic, and Pacific oceans.

- These fish have flat bodies with long fins and small mouths. Their patterns change as the fish get older.

Freshwater fish

Freshwater fish live in rivers, streams, and lakes. There are very few fish that can live in both freshwater and saltwater.

Piranhas

- Piranhas live in the lakes and rivers of South America and grow to 2 feet long.

- They hunt in packs and attack other animals, using their razor-sharp teeth to bite out lumps of meat.

The teeth in a piranha's mouth slice together like a pair of scissors.

Catfish

- Catfish have feelers that stick out from around their mouths. These feelers look like cats' whiskers and are called barbels.

- Catfish use these barbels to find food that is hidden in the mud of riverbeds.

200

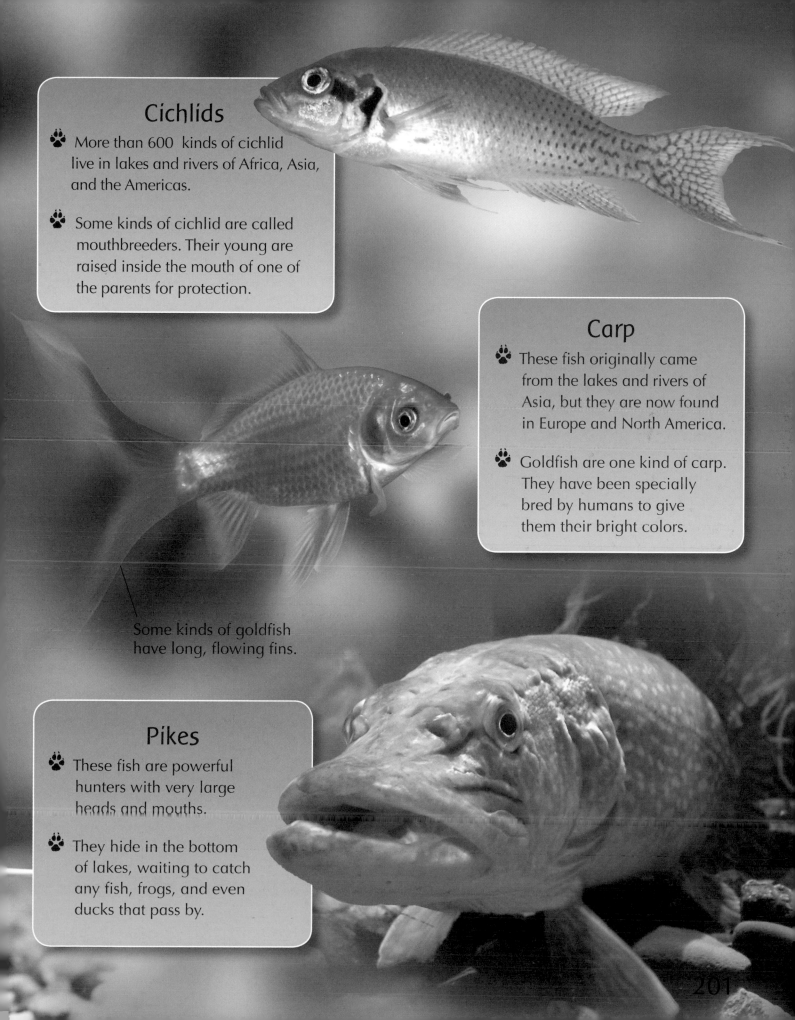

Cichlids

- More than 600 kinds of cichlid live in lakes and rivers of Africa, Asia, and the Americas.

- Some kinds of cichlid are called mouthbreeders. Their young are raised inside the mouth of one of the parents for protection.

Carp

- These fish originally came from the lakes and rivers of Asia, but they are now found in Europe and North America.

- Goldfish are one kind of carp. They have been specially bred by humans to give them their bright colors.

Some kinds of goldfish have long, flowing fins.

Pikes

- These fish are powerful hunters with very large heads and mouths.

- They hide in the bottom of lakes, waiting to catch any fish, frogs, and even ducks that pass by.

201

Amphibians

Amphibians are animals that spend their adult lives on land but return to the water to lay their eggs. Their young grow up in the water, but they move onto land when they are adults.

Poison arrow frogs

🐾 These frogs are small, but they are very poisonous. Their bright colors warn other animals to stay away.

🐾 They live in the forests of South America, hunting insects and other small creatures.

Newts

🐾 Newts have long, thin bodies with long tails that are flattened from top to bottom.

🐾 If a newt loses a leg or even an eye, it can grow back the missing body part. This is called regeneration.

Toads

- There are about 300 species, or kinds, of toad. They eat insects and other small animals, which they catch with their tongues.

- Some kinds of toad make a poison that can paralyze and even kill an attacker.

Salamanders

- Salamanders are closely related to newts. They live in rivers, lakes, and woodlands in cool parts of the world.

- The largest salamander is the giant salamander. It can grow to a length of 5 feet.

Frogs

- Frogs have long legs that are ideal for leaping, as well as webbed feet that are good for swimming.

- They have smooth skin and leap around, while toads have skin with warts and hop.

203

Reptiles

Reptiles are animals that have scaly skin. Some kinds of reptile spend a lot of time in water, but they all have to lay their eggs on land.

Turtles

🐾 Turtles can pull their heads and legs inside their hard shells for protection from attackers.

🐾 Turtles are found in lakes and rivers and in warm seas. Some sea turtles can swim huge distances, covering 300 miles in just 10 days.

Crocodiles tuck their legs into their sides when they swim through the water.

Alligators

🐾 These reptiles have long bodies with short legs and long tails, which they flick to push them through the water. They eat fish, small mammals, and birds.

🐾 Alligators have wide snouts, while crocodiles usually have narrow snouts.

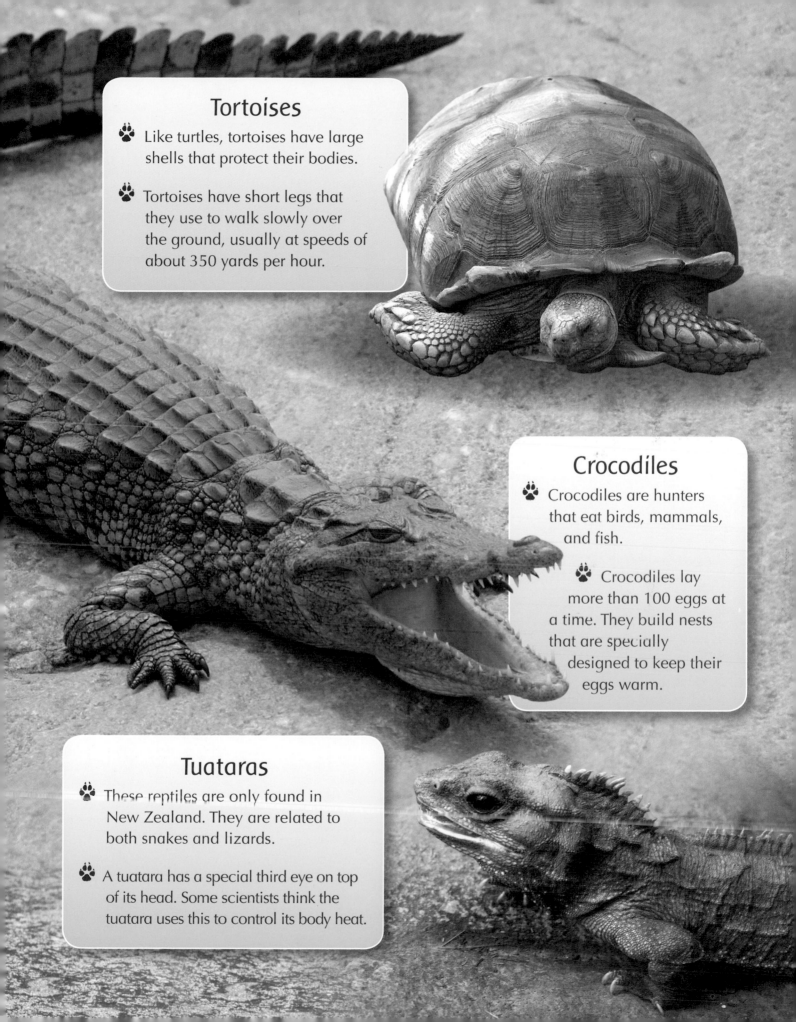

Tortoises

🐾 Like turtles, tortoises have large shells that protect their bodies.

🐾 Tortoises have short legs that they use to walk slowly over the ground, usually at speeds of about 350 yards per hour.

Crocodiles

🐾 Crocodiles are hunters that eat birds, mammals, and fish.

🐾 Crocodiles lay more than 100 eggs at a time. They build nests that are specially designed to keep their eggs warm.

Tuataras

🐾 These reptiles are only found in New Zealand. They are related to both snakes and lizards.

🐾 A tuatara has a special third eye on top of its head. Some scientists think the tuatara uses this to control its body heat.

More reptiles

Boas and pythons

- These large snakes eat birds and mammals. They kill their prey by wrapping their bodies around the animals so tightly that the prey cannot breathe. This is called constriction.

- When the prey is dead, these snakes open their mouths very wide and swallow the animals whole.

Poisonous snakes

- There are nearly 3,000 kinds of snake, of which about 450 make poison. They use this poison to kill prey and to defend themselves.

- Most poisonous snakes inject poison by biting. But one kind, the spitting cobra, squirts poison at the eyes of attackers. This can blind attackers, letting the cobras escape.

The Indian cobra has a hood that it stretches out when threatened to scare off an attacker.

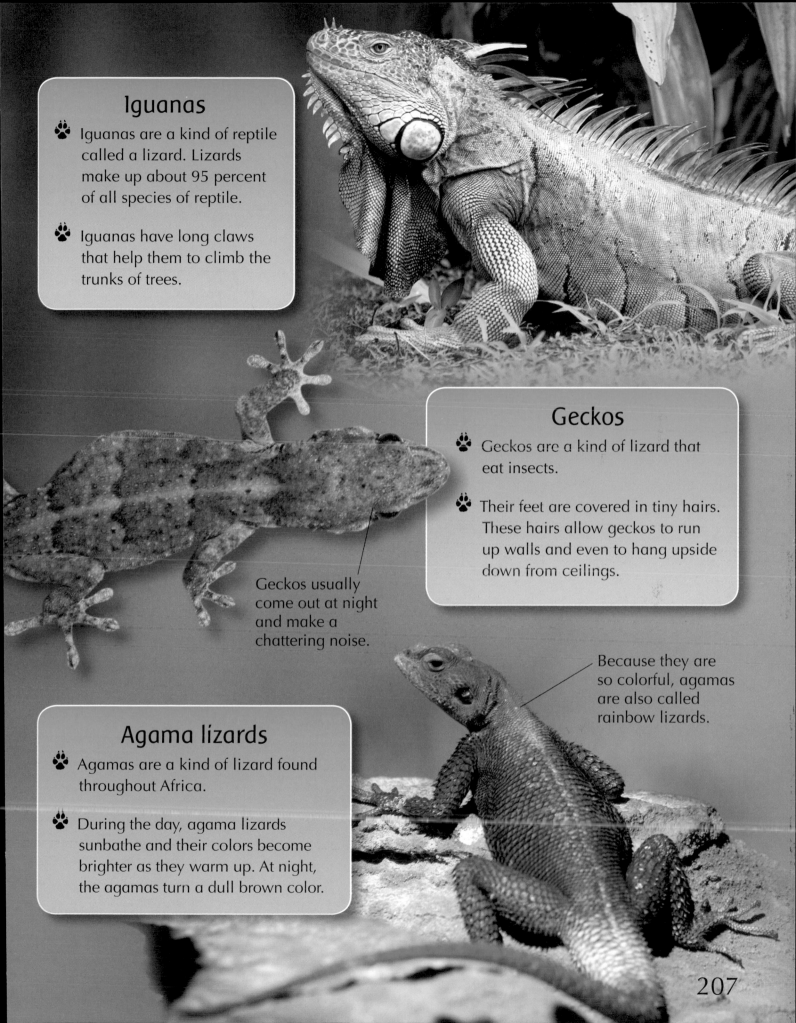

Iguanas

- Iguanas are a kind of reptile called a lizard. Lizards make up about 95 percent of all species of reptile.

- Iguanas have long claws that help them to climb the trunks of trees.

Geckos

- Geckos are a kind of lizard that eat insects.

- Their feet are covered in tiny hairs. These hairs allow geckos to run up walls and even to hang upside down from ceilings.

Geckos usually come out at night and make a chattering noise.

Because they are so colorful, agamas are also called rainbow lizards.

Agama lizards

- Agamas are a kind of lizard found throughout Africa.

- During the day, agama lizards sunbathe and their colors become brighter as they warm up. At night, the agamas turn a dull brown color.

207

Birds

Birds are animals that lay eggs and whose bodies are covered in feathers. All birds have two wings— even the ones that cannot fly.

Egret

Herons

🐾 Herons belong to a group of birds that includes egrets.

🐾 They are wading birds and have long legs so that they can stand in water looking for fish.

If attacked, an ostrich can kick its long legs to defend itself.

Flightless birds

🐾 There are several kinds of bird that do not fly. They include penguins and emus.

🐾 Ostriches are the world's largest birds. They have very long legs and can run up to 40 miles per hour.

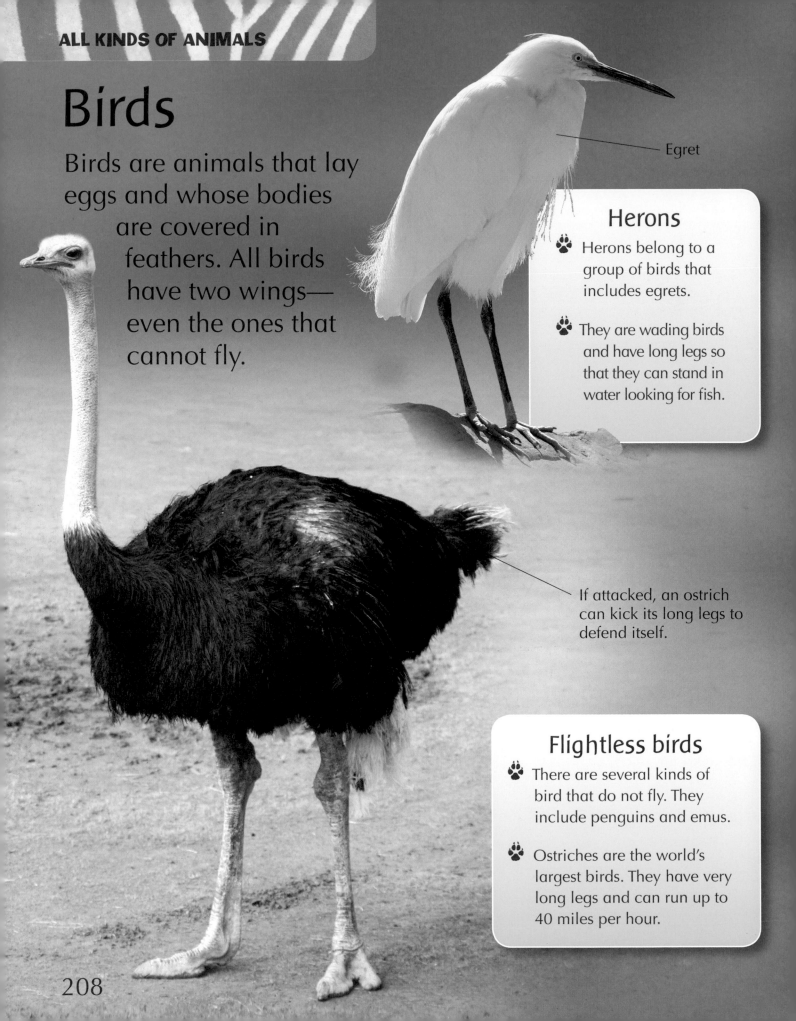

Pelicans

 Pelicans have long beaks with pouches underneath. They use these pouches to scoop fish out of the water.

 Brown pelicans catch fish by diving from the air into a group of fish underwater.

Gulls

 There are 40 species, or kinds, of these large, web-footed seabirds.

 They hunt for food on beaches, eating worms, shellfish, and even human garbage. Larger gulls will steal eggs and young from other birds to eat.

Gulls use their large wings to glide through the air.

Swans use their long necks to reach down to the riverbed to eat pondweed.

Wildfowl

 Birds in this group include ducks, qeese, and swans. All of these birds have webbed feet, and they can swim and float on water.

 Their feathers are covered in an oil that stops them from absorbing water. This would cause the birds to sink.

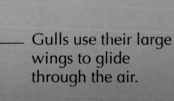

More birds

Kingfishers sit on branches over streams, looking for fish to catch in the water below.

Kingfishers

- Kingfishers are birds with large heads and long, pointed beaks. They mainly eat fish, which they catch by plunging into the water.

- There are some 90 different species, or kinds, of kingfisher found around the world.

Blackbirds puff out their feathers to make themselves look bigger when they are threatened.

Songbirds

- There are about 4,000 species of birds that sing. Their songs range from the tuneful calls of blackbirds to the squawks of crows.

- The birds use these songs to attract partners and to defend the areas they live in.

Parrots

- This group of birds includes macaws, cockatoos, parakeets, and budgerigars.

- Many kinds of parrot can copy human speech and say simple phrases.

Hummingbirds

- Hummingbirds are the only birds that can fly backward.

- They use their long beaks to reach the sugary nectar found in flowers.

The hyacinth macaw is the largest kind of flying parrot.

This falcon has very good eyesight and can see prey moving from great distances.

Birds of prey

- These are powerful birds, with hooked beaks and feet that end in sharp claws called talons.

- Birds of prey include eagles, falcons, and owls. They eat other animals, including small mammals and fish.

11

Mammals

Mammals are animals whose bodies are covered in fur. Most of them give birth to live young instead of laying eggs. Female mammals then make milk to feed their young.

Pouch

Platypus

- The platypus is unusual because it is a mammal that lays eggs.

- It has a ducklike beak and webbed feet to help it swim. It also has small poisonous spurs on its back legs to defend itself with.

Kangaroos

- Kangaroos belong to a group of mammals called marsupials. Female marsupials have pouches to carry their young around in.

- There are over 300 kinds of marsupial, including koalas and opossums.

212

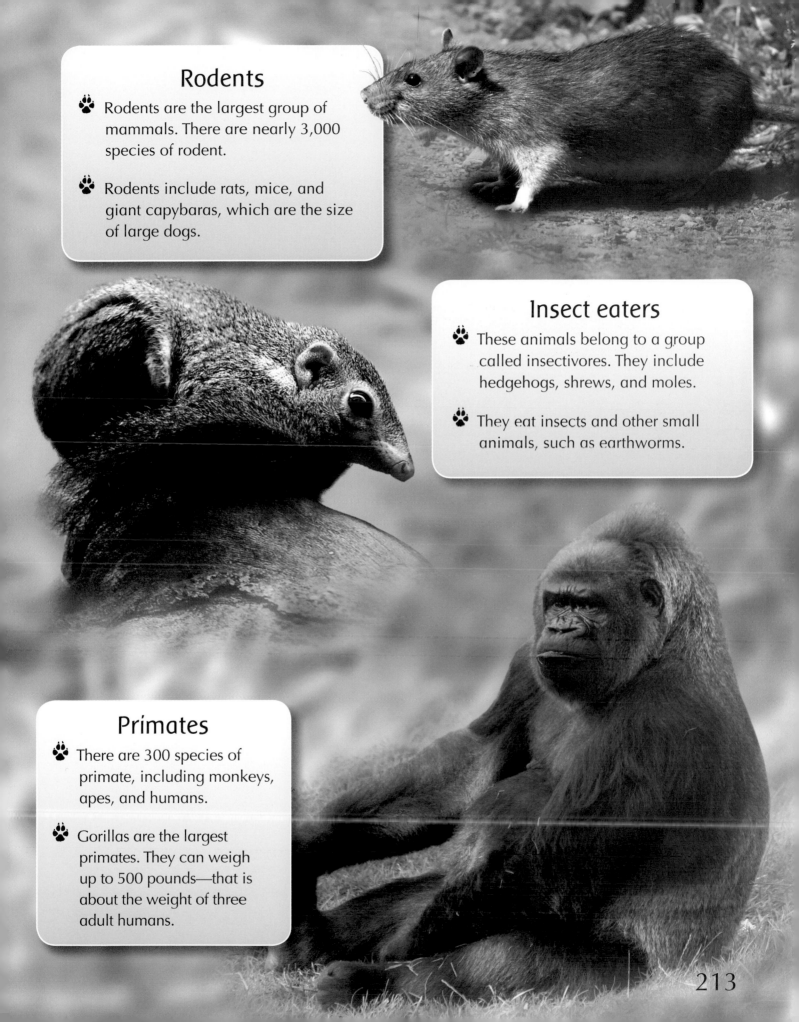

Rodents

🐾 Rodents are the largest group of mammals. There are nearly 3,000 species of rodent.

🐾 Rodents include rats, mice, and giant capybaras, which are the size of large dogs.

Insect eaters

🐾 These animals belong to a group called insectivores. They include hedgehogs, shrews, and moles.

🐾 They eat insects and other small animals, such as earthworms.

Primates

🐾 There are 300 species of primate, including monkeys, apes, and humans.

🐾 Gorillas are the largest primates. They can weigh up to 500 pounds—that is about the weight of three adult humans.

213

More mammals

Whales flick their tails up and down to push them through the water.

Whales

- Whales belong to a group of mammals called cetaceans. They have long, fishlike bodies and their front legs have become flippers.

- A blue whale needs to eat nearly 4 tons of krill every day—that is nearly the weight of three family cars.

Rhinoceros

- Rhinos are mammals with hooves and one or two horns just above their noses.

- There are five kinds, or species, of rhino living in Africa, India, and South-east Asia.

Rhinos have a thick skin called a hide.

Lions

- Lions belong to a group of mammals, called carnivores.

- They have stabbing teeth and long claws. Male lions have thick manes of hair around their heads and necks.

Mane

Deer

- There are about 30 different species of deer. They are all plant eaters and feed on grass, twigs, bark, and plant shoots.

- The largest deer are moose, which can grow to more than 7 feet in height.

Bears

- There are nine species of bear, including polar bears, grizzly bears, brown bears, and sun bears.

- Most bears are carnivores, or meat eaters, but they will also eat ants, seeds, bees, nuts, and berries.

Some useful words

❀ Aquatic
Something that lives in water.

❀ Behavior
All the actions of an animal, such as the way it feeds and moves.

❀ Bird
An animal with a backbone that has a body covered in feathers and has wings instead of arms.

❀ Camouflage
Coloring that allows an animal to blend in with its background.

❀ Colony
A group of animals living together in a shared home.

❀ Canopy
The leaves and branches of trees that form a covering or layer over the rest of the forest.

❀ Carnivore
An animal that eats meat.

❀ Caterpillar
The name given to the larva of a butterfly or moth.

❀ Conifer
A tree that has needle-shaped leaves.

❀ Crustacean
An animal without a backbone that has a body covered by an outer skeleton.

❀ Deciduous
Plants that drop their leaves at a certain time of year and then grow a new set.

❀ Desert
An area where very little rain falls. Few animals and plants can survive in a desert.

❀ Dung
Droppings produced by animals.

❀ Endangered
A species, or kind, of animal that is so few in number that it is in danger of disappearing completely.

❀ Equator
An imaginary line that runs around the middle of the earth.

❀ Estuary
A place where a river meets the sea and where saltwater mixes with freshwater.

❧ Extinct

An animal or plant species that no longer exists.

❧ Fin

A part of the body of a fish that is used for swimming.

❧ Gills

The parts used by fish and some other aquatic animals to help them breathe under water.

❧ Glide

To move through the air with little effort.

❧ Grassland

A type of habitat that is dominated by grasses and has very few trees.

❧ Habitat

The name given to the place where an animal or plant lives.

❧ Herbivore

An animal that eats plants.

❧ Hibernation

A type of deep sleep that allows some animals to survive a cold winter.

❧ Hover

To stay in one place in the air. Hummingbirds hover by moving their wings backward and forward.

❧ Incubation

Keeping eggs warm so that they will hatch successfully.

❧ Insect

An animal without a backbone that has three body parts, three pairs of legs, and usually two pairs of wings.

❧ Invertebrate

An animal that does not have a backbone.

❧ Larva

The young of insects and other invertebrates. For example, the larva of a butterfly is a caterpillar.

❧ Mammal

An animal with a backbone that usually has hair on its skin. Female mammals make milk to feed their young.

❧ Mangrove

Trees that grow along muddy coastlines in warm parts of the world.

❧ Metamorphosis

A change in body shape that occurs when a larva grows into an adult.

❧ Microscopic

Too small to be seen with the naked eye.

❧ Migration

A regular journey made by an animal.

Mollusk
An animal with a soft body, usually with an outer shell.

Nocturnal
When an animal is active at night and rests during the day.

Plankton
The tiny plants and animals that are found floating close to the surface of ponds, lakes, and seas.

Poisonous
Something that produces poison.

Polar
To do with the areas around the North and South Poles.

Predator
An animal that hunts and feeds on other animals.

Preen
To clean feathers.

Prey
An animal that is hunted by other animals.

Recycle
To use something again, such as paper or glass bottles.

Reproduce
To produce young.

Reptile
An animal with a backbone that has four legs and a body covered by scales. Female reptiles lay leathery eggs.

Savanna
Another name given to grasslands found in warm parts of the world.

Scale
A small, platelike structure that is found on the skin of reptiles and fish.

Scavenger
An animal that feeds on dead animals.

School
A group of fish that swim together.

Sense organ
Part of the nervous system that can detect changes in the surroundings, such as eyes and ears.

Skeleton
The framework of a body, that holds it together. Some skeletons are inside bodies, while others are outside.

Slime
A slippery substance.

Streamlined

When something is smooth and tapered and can move through water or air with very little effort.

Talons

The name given to the large claws of birds of prey.

Temperate

Areas of the world that have a mild climate and four seasons.

Tentacle

A long, feeler-like structure found on certain animals, such as anemones and squid.

Tropical

Areas of the world that lie near the equator, around the middle of the Earth, and are hot all year round.

Tusk

An extra-long tooth found on some animals, such as elephants and warthogs.

Venom

A harmful liquid that some animals make to kill prey or to defend themselves.

Vertebrate

An animal that has a backbone.

Water hole

A hollow in the ground where water collects and remains for much of the year.

Waterproof

A surface that keeps water out.

Wilderness

A wild place that has not been changed by people.

WEBLINKS

Parragon does not accept responsibility for the content of any websites mentioned in this publication. If you have any queries about their content, please refer to the organization that produced the web site. If you are under 18, the websites mentioned should only be used with the involvement of a parent or guardian.

http://nationalzoo.si.edu/
The National Zoological Park of the USA and part of the Smithsonian Institution.

http://www.amnh.org/
The American Museum of Natural History in New York City.

http://www.panda.org/
The WWF (formerly the World Wildlife Fund).

http://kids.nationalgeographic.com/
Children's section of National Geographic.

http://animal.discovery.com/
Animals section of the Discovery channel.

http://www.fws.gov/endangered/kids/
The US Fish and Wildlife Service.

Index

A

African wild dog 43
alligators 170, 204
amphibians 16, 130, 134, 178, 202–203
angelfish 128, 199
anglerfish 165
animal behavior 14–15
Antarctica 49, 88–91
antelopes 20, 21, 56
anthias 154
ants 34, 35, 185
arachnids 192–193
Arctic 82–87
Arctic tern 85
arthropods 13, 184
Atacama Desert 48

B

babies 11, 16, 17, 59, 162
    chicks 114–115
bacteria 21
badgers 58, 63
bald eagle 108–109
barnacles 143
barracudas 160
bats 96, 116–119
beaches 146–147
bears 133, 215
    brown bears 76–77
    polar bears 86–87
bees 93, 121, 186
beetles 70, 187
bighorn sheep 100
bird watching 172

birds 104–115, 208–211
    beaks 28, 29, 104, 109, 141
    eggs 11, 16, 114
    flightless 110–111, 208
    forest 66, 69, 75, 78–79
    migrating 73
    nests 64, 67, 71, 95, 109, 112–113
    river birds 137, 138
    skeleton 12, 179
    songbirds 31, 210
    waders 140–141, 151
    wings 106–107
birds of prey 43, 79, 104, 108, 211
birth 11, 16, 17, 212
bison 60–61, 174
bivalves 139, 153
blennies 143
blue jays 75
blue tits 69
boas 206
body parts 12–13, 179
breathing 10
brittlestars 167
brown bears 76–77
budding 17
burrowing owl 63
butterflies 92, 184
    life cycle 122–123

C

camels 54–55
camouflage 29, 68, 71
canopy 26, 28–29, 32
caribou 84
carnivores 10, 21
carp 201

cassowaries 111
caterpillars 68, 69, 122
catfish 200
cave fish 97
caves 96–97
centipedes 19, 190
chameleons 28, 29
cheetahs 42, 43
chimpanzees 15
cicadas 30
cichlids 131, 201
cities 19, 94–95
clams 153, 194
climate change 23, 170
clownfish 155
cobras 206
cockles 139
cockroaches 185
color 14
communicating 14, 30–31, 57
conservation 172–173
coral reefs 152–155
corals 179
cormorants 110, 138
coyotes 57
crabs 13, 139, 145, 150, 167, 188
crocodiles 170, 205
crustaceans 188–189
cuckoos 114
curlews 140
cuttlefish 157, 194

D

deciduous trees 66
deer 72, 74, 84, 215
deltas 138
deserts 25, 48–55

223

Acknowledgments

All artwork supplied by Myke Taylor, The Art Agency

Photo credits:
Cover: Elephant: Martin Harvey:Gallo Images/Corbis. Parrot: Theo Allofs/Corbis. Giraffe: Martin Harvey/Corbis.
1 Dreamstime.com/David Davis, 2–3 Corbis/Kevin Schafer, 4t Dreamstime.com/Richard Gunion, 5br Dreamstime.com/Asther Lau Choon Siew, 6tl Dreamstime.com/Kiyoshi Takahase Segundo, 6tr Dreamstime.com/Fred Goldstein, 6ml Dreamstime.com/Carolyne Pehora, 6-7m Digital Vision, 6t Dreamstime.com/Ian Scott, 7tr Dreamstime.com/Sanja Stepanovic, 7b Dreamstime.com/Wei Send Chen, 8-9 Corbis/Gallo Images, 10bl Dreamstime.com/Johannes Gerhardus Swanepoel, 11tr Dreamstime.com/Vaida Petreikiene, 11m Dreamstime.com, 11b Dreamstime.com/Stephen Inglis, 12br Dreamstime.com, 12-13 Dreamstime.com/Andre Nantel, 13t Dreamstime.com/Radu Razvan, 13m Dreamstime.com/Vladimir Ivanov, 14tl Dreamstime.com, 14b Dreamstime.com/Mark Karasek, 15tr Dreamstime.com/Vladimir Kindrachov, 15b Dreamstime.com, 16t Dreamstime.com/Tomas Hajek, 16b Dreamstime.com, 17m Dreamstime.com, 17b Dreamstime.com/Steffen Foerster, 18 Dreamstime.com/Stuart Elflett, 18b Dreamstime.com/George Bailey, 19t Dreamstime.com/Bartlomiej Kwieciszewski, 19m Dreamstime.com, 19b Dreamstime.com, 20m Dreamstime.com/Anna Kowalska, 20bl Dreamstime.com, 21br Dreamstime.com, 22t Dreamstime.com/David Hyde, 22b Digital Vision, 23t Digital Vision, 23b Digital Vision, 24-25 Corbis/Kennan Ward, 26t Tall Tree Ltd, 26b Dreamstime.com, 27t Tall Tree Ltd, 27m Dreamstime.com, 28tl Dreamstime.com/Phil Date, 28br Dreamstime.com/Kathy Wynn, 29tr Dreamstime.com , 29m Tall Tree Ltd, 29b Dreamstime.com/Michael Ledray, 30tl Dreamstime.com, 30br Dreamstime.com/Christopher Marin, 31t Dreamstime.com/David Davis, 31b Dreamstime.com, 32–33 Dreamstime.com, 33br Dreamstime.com, 34t Tall Tree Ltd, 34b Dreamstime.com/Mike Evans, 35t Dreamstime.com/Ferenc Cegledi, 35b Dreamstime.com, 36b Dreamstime.com, 37tr Dreamstime.com/Graça Victoria, 37m Dreamstime.com/Tze Roung Tan, 38–39 Dreamstime.com/Stefan Ekernas, 38bl Dreamstime.com, 39m Digital Vision, 39r Dreamstime.com, 40b Dreamstime.com/Andre Maritz, 40–41 Dreamstime.com, 41t Dreamstime.com, 41br Dreamstime.com/Steffen Foerster, 42–43 Corbis, 42b Digital Vision, 43tr Dreamstime.com, 43br Dreamstime.com, 44tl Dreamstime.com/Michael Pettigrew, 44–45 Dreamstime.com/Craig Ruaux, 45r Digital Vision, 46–47 Dreamstime.com/Chris Fourie, 46b Dreamstime.com/Steve Meyfroidt, 47t Dreamstime.com, 47b Dreamstime.com/Laura Frankel, 48–49 Dreamstime.com/Vladimir Pomortsev, 48b Dreamstime.com/Michael Schofield, 49t Dreamstime.com, 49b Dreamstime.com/Alexander Putyata, 50tl Dreamstime.com/Steve Schowiak, 50b Dreamstime.com/Vladimir Pomortsev, 51t Dreamstime.com, 51b Digital Vision, 52-53 Dreamstime.com, 53t Dreamstime.com/Stephen McSweeny, 54 Dreamstime.com/Dario Diament, 55t Dreamstime.com/Julija Mezecka, 55b Dreamstime.com/Keith Naylor, 56–57 Dreamstime.com/Tyler Olson, 56b Dreamstime.com/Michael West, 57b Dreamstime.com/Ken Griffith, 58t Digital Vision, 58b Dreamstime.com/Joe Gough, 59t Dreamstime.com, 59b Dreamstime.com/Andreas Steinbach, 60–61 Dreamstime.com, 61t Dreamstime.com, 61br Dreamstime.com, 62tl Dreamstime.com/Bob Wolverton, 63m Dreamstime.com/Gary Unwin, 63b Dreamstime.com/Pavel Gribkov, 64 tl Dreamstime.com, 64br Dreamstime.com, 65 t Dreamstime.com, 65b Dreamstime.com/Ruta Saulyte-laurinaviciene, 66tl Digital Vision, 66bl Digital Vision, 67t Dreamstime.com/Robert Hambley, 67b Dreamstime.com/Jorge Felix Costa, 68t Dreamstime.com/Martina Berg, 68b Dreamstime.com/Gumenuk Vitalij, 69 Dreamstime.com/Edite Artmann, 70tl Dreamstime.com/Gumenuk Vitalij, 70br Dreamstime.com, 71t Dreamstime.com/Michael Pettigrew, 71b Corbis/Roger Tidman, 72tr Dreamstime.com, 72b Dreamstime.com/Bruce Macqueen, 73tr Dreamstime.com, 73br Dreamstime.com, 74b Dreamstime.com/Tony Campbell, 75t Digital Vision, 75mr Dreamstime.com/Robert Hambley, 75br Dreamstime.com, 76 Dreamstime.com, 77 Dreamstime.com/Ryhor Zasinets, 78tl Dreamstime.com, 78br Dreamstime.com, 79tl Dreamstime.com/Bruce Macqueen, 79br Dreamstime.com, 80tl Dreamstime.com/Sergey Anatolievich, 80m Dreamstime.com/Gail Johnson, 80bl Dreamstime.com/Sergey Anatolievich, 81t Dreamstime.com/Aaron Whitney, 81b Dreamstime.com/Maggie Dziadkiewicz, 82t Dreamstime.com/Anthony Hathaway, 82b Dreamstime.com/Steffen Foerster, 83t Dreamstime.com, 83b Dreamstime.com/Holger Wulschlaeger, 84bl Dreamstime.com/Geoffrey Kuchera, 84–85 Dreamstime.com/Lauren Jones, 85t Dreamstime.com/Roy Longmuir, 86 Dreamstime.com/Carolyne Pehora, 87t Dreamstime.com/Anthony Hathaway, 87b Dreamstime.com/Kathleen Struckle, 88t Dreamstime.com/Alexander Putyata, 88b Dreamstime.com/Jan Will, 88t Dreamstime.com/Alexander Putyata, 88b Dreamstime.com/Bernard Breton, 90b Dreamstime.com/Bernard Breton, 91t Dreamstime.com/Bernard Breton, 91b Dreamstime.com/Neil Wigmore, 92t Dreamstime.com/Peter Mautsch, 92bl Dreamstime.com/Martina Berg, 92br Dreamstime.com, 93tr Dreamstime.com/Richard McDowell, 93bl Dreamstime.com/Marilyn Barbone, 94t Tall Tree Ltd, 94b Dreamstime.com/Nicola Gavin, 95t Dreamstime.com/Xavier Marchant, 95ml Dreamstime.com/Wael Hamdan, 95br Dreamstime.com/Piotr Bieniecki, 96 Dreamstime.com, 97br Corbis/DK Limited, 98m Dreamstime.com/Glen Gaffney, 98b Dreamstime.com, 99tl Dreamstime.com/Mike Carlson, 99br Dreamstime.com/Vladimir Pomortsev, 100 Dreamstime.com/Rick Parsons, 101tl Dreamstime.com/Keith Yong, 101tr Dreamstime.com/Kaleb Timberlake, 101br Dreamstime.com/Sascha Burkard, 102-103 Corbis/Steve Kaufman, 104bl Digital Vision, 104m Digital Vision, 105t Dreamstime.com, 105b Dreamstime.com/John Sfondilias, 106 Digital Vision, 107tr Dreamstime.com/Willie Manalo, 107tl Digital Vision, 107br Dreamstime.com/Kiyoshi Takahase Segundo, 108t Dreamstime.com/Robert Cocquyt, 109t Dreamstime.com/Matt Ragen, 109b Dreamstime.com/Stephen Inglis, 110t Digital Vision, 110b Dreamstime.com/Roy Longmuir, 111br Dreamstime.com/Linda Bucklin, 112tl Digital Vision, 112b Dreamstime.com/Ivan Chuyev, 113tl Dreamstime.com/Vaida Petreikiene, 113br Digital Vision, 114m Dreamstime.com/Scott Impink, 114bl Dreamstime.com/Johannes Gerhardus Swanepoel, 115tr Digital Vision, 115b Digital Vision, 116 Corbis, 117tr Dreamstime.com/Angela Farley, 117ml Dreamstime.com, 117bl Dreamstime.com/Paul Cowan, 118tl Dreamstime.com/Geza Farkas, 119 Dreamstime.com/Adam Booth, 120tr Digital Vision, 120b Dreamstime.com/Bobby Deal, 121tr Dreamstime.com/Fred Goldstein, 121br Dreamstime.com/Sanja Stepanovic, 122-123 Dreamstime.com/Elaine Davis, 122b Dreamstime.com, 123b Dreamstime.com/Geza Farkas, 124tr Dreamstime.com/Nico Smit, 125r Dreamstime.com/Alice Dehaven, 126–127 Corbis/Jeffrey L. Rotman, 128m Dreamstime.com/Ellen McIlroy, 129r Digital Vision, 129b Dreamstime.com, 130t Dreamstime.com/Mike Brake, 130b Dreamstime.com/Michael L., 131t Dreamstime.com/Dallas Powell, jr., 131b Dreamstime.com/Holger Leyrer, 132b Dreamstime.com/Daniel Slocum, 133t Dreamstime.com/Michael Thompson, 133b Dreamstime.com/David Hyde, 134–135 Dreamstime.com/Andrei Contiu, 134b Dreamstime.com/Bruce MacQueen, 136t Dreamstime.com/Chris Schlosser, 136b Corbis/Dale C. Spartas, 137tl Dreamstime.com/Richard Merwin, 137b Digital Vision, 138 tl NASA, 138bl Dreamstime.com/Anita Huszti, 139m Dreamstime.com/Sergey Khachatryan, 139br Dreamstime.com/Joseph Helfenberger, 140tr Dreamstime.com/Caroline Henri, 140b Digital Vision, 141tl Dreamstime.com/Stefan Ekernas, 141br Dreamstime.com/Christina Craft, 142 iStockphoto.com, 142b Dreamstime.com/Jamie Wilson, 143t Dreamstime.com/Stuart Key, 143b Dreamstime.com/Uwe Ohse, 144 Dreamstime.com, 145tr Dreamstime.com/Asther Lau Choon Siew, 145ml Dreamstime.com/Asther Lau Choon Siew, 145br Dreamstime.com/Daniela Spyropoulou, 147t Dreamstime.com, 147br Dreamstime.com/Jay Prescott, 148t Dreamstime.com/Jeff Waibel, 148b Dreamstime.com, 149tr Dreamstime.com, 149br Dreamstime.com, 150t Dreamstime.com/Daniel Gustavsson, 150b Dreamstime.com/Anthony Hall, 151r Dreamstime.com/Humberto Ortega, 152–153 Dreamstime.com/Matthias Weinrich, 152bl Dreamstime.com/Asther Lau Choon Siew, 152br Dreamstime.com/Asther Lau Choon Siew, 153t Dreamstime.com/Ian Scott, 153b Dreamstime.com/Asther Lau Choon Siew, 154t Dreamstime.com/Asther Lau Choon Siew, 154b Dreamstime.com/Ian Scott, 155m Dreamstime.com/Wei Send Chen, 155b Dreamstime.com/Andrea Leone, 156t Dreamstime.com/Harald Bolten, 157t Dreamstime.com/Jeremy Bruskotter, 157m Dreamstime.com, 157b Dreamstime.com, 159b Corbis, 160 Dreamstime.com/Asther Lau Choon Siew, 161t Dreamstime.com/Steve Weaver, 161b Dreamstime.com/Ian Scott, 162–163 Dreamstime.com/Brett Atkins, 163t Dreamstime.com/Jason Vandehey, 163br Digital Vision, 168-169 Dreamstime.com/Wang Sanjun, 170 Dreamstime.com/Fah mun Kwan, 171br Dreamstime.com/Nico Smit, 172tr Dreamstime.com/Steven Pike, 172b Dreamstime.com/Steffen Foerster, 173t Digital Vision, 173b Dreamstime.com/John Bloor, 174tr Dreamstime.com/Anthony Hathaway, 174bl Dreamstime.com/Jostein Hauge, 175t iStockphoto.com, 175br Dreamstime.com/Ethan Kocak, 176–177 Corbis/Kevin Schafer, 178 Dreamstime.com/Anthony Hathaway, 179t all Dreamstime.com, 179b Dreamstime.com, 180t Dreamstime.com/Robert Gubiani, 180b Dreamstime.com/Dennis Sabo, 181t Dreamstime.com/Cathy Figuli, 181m Dreamstime.com, 181b Dreamstime.com/Asther Lau Choon Siew, 182t Dreamstime.com/Dusty Cline, 184t Dreamstime.com/Carolina K. Smith m.d., 184b Dreamstime.com/Richard Gunion, 185t Dreamstime.com/Joao Estevao Andrade de Freitas, 185m Dreamstime.com/Paul Cowan, 185b Dreamstime.com/Marek Kosmal, 186t Dreamstime.com/Marie Jeanne, 186b Digital Vision, 187t Dreamstime.com/Frederic Roux, 187m Dreamstime.com/Oleksiy Lebedynskiy, 187b Dreamstime.com, 188t Dreamstime.com/Nico Smit, 188b Dreamstime.com, 189t Dreamstime.com/Simone van den Berg, 189b Dreamstime.com/Uzi Hen, 190t Dreamstime.com/Joao Estevao Andrade de Freitas, 191t Dreamstime.com/Wichittra Srisunon, 192t Dreamstime.com/Fulvio Evangelista, 192b Dreamstime.com/Dawn Allyn, 193t Dreamstime.com/Caroline Henri, 193b Dreamstime.com, 194t Dreamstime.com/Rayna Canedy, 194b Dreamstime.com/Asther Lau Choon Siew, 195t Dreamstime.com/Tom Davison, 195m Dreamstime.com/Asther Lau Choon Siew, 195b Dreamstime.com/Martina Misar, 196t Dreamstime.com/Asther Lau Choon Siew, 196b Dreamstime.com/Asther Lau Choon Siew, 197t Dreamstime.com/Robert Daniels, 197m Dreamstime.com/Kelly Bates, 197b Dreamstime.com/James Hearn, 198t Dreamstime.com/Ian Scott, 198b Dreamstime.com/Asther Lau Choon Siew, 199t Dreamstime.com/John Abramo, 199m Dreamstime.com/Johnny Lye, 199b Dreamstime.com/Asther Lau Choon Siew, 200t Dreamstime.com/Pamela Hodson, 200b Dreamstime.com/Feng Yu, 201t Dreamstime.com/Dallas Powell, jr., 201m Dreamstime.com/Heidi Hart, 201b Dreamstime.com/Tim Haynes, 202tl Dreamstime.com/Steffen Foerster, 202b Dreamstime.com/Holger Leyrer, 203t Dreamstime.com/Dmitrii Korovin, 203m Dreamstime.com/Anita Huszti, 203b Dreamstime.com/Lukáš Hejtman, 204tl Dreamstime.com/Hannu Liivaar, 204b Dreamstime.com/Paul Wolf, 205t Dreamstime.com/Darren Baker, 205m Dreamstime.com/Gert Very, 205b Dreamstime.com/Andy Heyward, 206tl Dreamstime.com, 206b Dreamstime.com, 207t Dreamstime.com/Michael Klenetsky, 207m Dreamtime.com/Alex Bramwell, 207b Dreamstime.com/Christian Kahler, 208t Dreamstime.com/Michael Johansson, 208b Dreamstime.com/Xavier Marchant, 209t Dreamstime.com/Laurin Rinder, 209m Dreamstime.com/Heather Craig, 209b Dreamstime.com, 210t Dreamstime.com/Johannes Gerhardus Swanepoel, 210b Dreamstime.com/Brian Lambert, 211tl Dreamstime.com/Kimberly Clark, 211tr Dreamstime.com/Olga Bogutyrenko, 211b Dreamstime.com/Nico Smit, 212b Dreamstime.com, 213t Dreamstime.com/Roger Whiteway, 213m Dreamstime.com, 213b Dreamstime.com/Martina Berg, 214b Dreamstime.com/Larry Powell, 215tr Dreamstime.com/Christine Mercer, 215m Digital Vision, 215b Dreamstime.com/William Sarver